Spiritual Warfare Ministries Presents:

Chains That Bind Generations

Breaking The Strongholds of
Generational Curses

Kenneth Scott

Scriptures in this publication are taken from the King James version of the Bible and paraphrased by the author.

Chains the Bind Generations
1st Printing

ISBN: 978-0-9796675-0-3

Copyright © 2007 by Kenneth Scott
Spiritual Warfare Ministries, Inc.
P.O. Box 2024
Birmingham, AL 35201-2024
(205) 853-9509

All rights reserved. Contents and/or cover of this book may not be reproduced or transmitted in any form or by any means, electronically or mechanically, without written permission from the author and publisher.

To request written permission to reproduce sections of this publication, write to:

Spiritual Warfare Ministries
Attention: Kenneth Scott
P.O. Box 2024
Birmingham, Alabama 35201-2024

(205) 853-9509

Contents

Chapter One—Do Generational Curses Still Exist?...... 7

Chapter Two—Personal Sin Curses 13

Chapter Three—The Famine 23

Chapter Four—The History 31

Chapter Five—Inherited Judgment............................. 39

Chapter Six—Inherited Giants 45

Chapter Seven—Generational Blessings 57

Chapter Eight—The Root Cause 63

Chapter Nine—Escaping the Gibeonites 81

Chapter Ten—Getting Released From the Curse 87

Chapter Eleven—The Atonement............................... 121

Chapter Twelve
—Implementing the Seven Sons of Saul 133

Preface

In 2 Samuel, chapter 21, David experienced a generational curse in his life. At first he thought his problems and difficulties were perhaps bad luck. But after they continued for three years in a row, he finally realized that there was more to his problems and difficulties than just bad luck. He eventually came to understand that he was under a generational curse. This curse was not caused by David's sins, but rather, the sins of those of a generation earlier who were now dead and gone.

Even though David had nothing at all to do with the sin that caused the curse, he and the Israelites were still being devastated by this curse. But David didn't just hope for the best and wait it out; he sought the face of the Lord for deliverance from the curse. It was then that the Lord gave him the answer. And, through the answer came their deliverance from the curse.

Some of our difficulties and struggles in life have come as a result of poor choices, decisions and undisciplined lifestyles. However, like David, some of our difficulties and struggles are not as a result of anything we have done at all. Some are as a result of the sins and transgressions of our ancestors. But just as David finally realized he was under a curse and sought the Lord for help and deliverance, we must do the same.

If you have been under a curse, you must come to understand that (just as God did for David), He has also made a way of escape for you out of your curse. As you read this book, be open, willing and obedient to the instructions of the Lord. And, as David escaped his curse, you will also be able to escape the curses of your life and receive God's blessings, favor and prosperity in life.

Chapter 1

Do Generational Curses Still Exist?

The Skeptics

There are many who do not believe that there is any validity to the teaching of generational curses. Those who do not believe in the Bible simply say that every man makes his own destiny. They also say that everything that happens good or bad in life simply happens by chance or the luck of the draw.

Those who believe in the Bible but do not believe in generational curses say that Christ has redeemed us from the curse of the law. And, since generational curses are actually curses, they believe that they are no longer applicable to us. They also say that when Christ came, He abolished the old law (Old Testament law), and we now only need to abide by the laws of the New Testament, thereby rendering the laws and doctrine of generational curses obsolete. This philosophy is doctrinal error. Let's establish this with the following passage:

> *Think not that I am come to destroy the law, or the prophets: I am not come to destroy, but to fulfil.*
> *Matthew 5:17*

The Fulfillment of the Law

In this passage, when Jesus said that He did not come to destroy *"the law"*, the *"law"* He is referring to is the Old Testament law. Now remember, the generational curse skeptics say that when Jesus came, He did away with or destroyed the Old Testament law. But in this passage Jesus is saying something completely different.

Jesus goes on to clarify that He did not come to destroy or do away with the Old law, but rather, *"to fulfill"* the law. What Jesus was actually saying was that He did *not* come to abolish the Old Testament law (this includes the law of generational curses), but to fulfill those laws that were only a picture and *shadow* of Him (Jesus Christ).

Two Types of Laws

All the laws in the Bible can be basically divided into two types of laws: prophetic laws and covenant laws. The prophetic laws were Old Testament laws that were given to serve only as a shadow or picture of Christ. The covenant laws were given in both the Old and New Testaments. They were not given solely as an example of Christ at all, but established laws by God for His people to obey throughout time. God established these laws for His people who were in covenant with Him to obey and keep them in His will.

The prophetic laws were different; they were only temporary. It's like when you see construction on the interstate and they post temporary speed limit signs in that particular zone. That's what the prophetic laws were like. Before Christ, the law was under construction. The prophetic laws were like that particular (temporary) zone of the whole law. It was established as a temporary law until the construction of Christ and the cross could be completed and fulfilled. But when Christ came and died, He completed the construction, fulfilling all the prophetic laws.

In this example about the interstate construction, once the construction is completed, the old, temporary speed limit signs (laws) are not completely abolished; they are only modified and replaced with new, current, more updated signs. In the same manner, God did not throw away or abolish the Old Testament laws. We still follow them as they relate to the law of the Spirit. The following is an example of a few of the prophetic laws:

Under the old prophetic law we needed a priest to go before us to make sacrifices unto the Lord. Under the new law we no longer need a priest to represent us and make sacrifices for us. Jesus Christ is now the High Priest who sits on the right hand of the Father making intercession for us.

Under the old prophetic law animal sacrifices were required to atone for our sins. We no longer have to make animal sacrifices anymore. Jesus became the final sacrificial lamb for all the sins of all mankind.

We no longer have to keep the Sabbath Day. When Christ died, He became our Sabbath (our place of rest). Whenever we are burdened or heavy laden, and we either do not come to Christ, or we go to something else for our rest or peace other than Christ, we now break the Sabbath day.

Under the old prophetic law, all the young men were circumcised on the eighth day. Any male who was not circumcised was considered an enemy of God. In addition, anyone living in the house of an uncircumcised male was also considered an enemy of God. Under the new law, the physical circumcision is no longer necessary. Circumcision is now a spiritual act. Circumcision is a cutting away of the flesh.

Spiritual circumcision is what happens when we receive Christ and allow His Spirit to fill us, and then lead and guide us. We cut away spiritual flesh, and allow the Spirit of Christ to lead us instead.

Again, these (prophetic) laws (like the example of the interstate construction) were not abolished at all; they were only altered as they related to the spiritual realm and with Christ.

But the covenant laws were not changed or altered at all. Examples of covenant laws are laws such as do not kill, steal, commit adultery, and others. Along with these covenant laws are also the laws of tithing, generational curses and many others. Jesus did not have to re-teach these laws in the New Testament because they were never changed or altered from the Old Testament. They are still just as relevant today as they were when God gave them.

Double Jeopardy

There are some who do not believe in generational curses because they say that all of our works and rewards will be settled in judgment. Now we all understand that we will either be rewarded or condemned in heaven for the life we lived on this earth. But we must also understand that there are physical rewards that will also be paid during our life here on earth for both good and bad. It's a type of double jeopardy.

In our legal court system we have a law called "Double Jeopardy." In the law of Double Jeopardy, a person cannot be tried for the same crime twice. After they are tried by a court of law and found innocent of a crime, they cannot be tried again for that same crime even if new evidence is found that clearly implicates them to actually be guilty beyond the shadow of a doubt.

Unfortunately, there is no such law with God. There is going to be a reward for the good, and consequences for the evil we do in our eternal life; but there are also going to be rewards and consequences paid in our earthly, physical lives for the same things. The punishments and penalties we suffer in the earth realm for our sins, unrighteousness and transgressions are actually generational curses and personal sin curses.

> *And Jesus answered and said, Verily I say unto you, There is no man that hath left house, or brethren, or sisters, or father, or mother, or wife, or children, or lands, for my sake, and the gospel's, but he shall receive an hundredfold <u>now in this time</u>, houses, and brethren, and sisters, and mothers, and children, and lands, with persecutions; <u>and in the world to come eternal life</u>.* —Mark 10:29-30

We often use this passage when referring to tithes and giving. We use it to show that if we give and serve the Lord, we will not only be blessed in heaven, but God will also bless us in our present, earthly life as well. Notice, the rewards He is referring to are based upon two time periods: "*in this time*" and "*in the world to come.*" It is obvious that when Jesus said "*in this time*" that He was referring to the present, physical, earthly life, and when He said, "*in the world to come*" He was referring to our eternal life.

So again, we would agree that He is talking about both a present, physical reward *and* an eternal reward for the work and sacrifices we make unto the Lord in this present life. If we can agree with this, wouldn't it stand to reason that if we can receive blessings for the good things we do in both the present and the after life, that it would also apply to the sinful and evil things we do as well? When we commit sin and transgress against God, instead of receiving the blessings, we receive the curse. These curses that are judged are called either personal sin curses or generational curses.

When I was a child, children not only received spankings (although we called them whippings at that time) from their parents, other adults who witnessed them misbehave could also spank them. An adult relative, teacher, or even a neighbor could see a child doing something mischievous and spank them for it. They would then call their parents and tell them, and later the child would also get another spanking for the exact same thing from their parents.

Some might feel that this type of double jeopardy punishment was cruel, but it actually helped. You may have heard the old adage that says, *"It takes a village to raise a child."* Parents are not always around to watch their children. But in those days the neighbors, other relatives, teachers and other adults in authority actually helped the parents to watch their children when the parents could not be around, thus helping to discipline and raise them better.

Anyway, back to the point I was making about the double spankings. Spiritually, there can be a type of double jeopardy punishment for us as well. As we said earlier, Jesus taught that we are going to receive an earthly reward as well as an eternal reward for the good or bad we do in this life. We can pay the penalty for our sins in this life (through personal sin curses or generational curses), and then turn around and pay a double jeopardy punishment for the same sins in the eternal life.

But again, thanks be to God for Jesus Christ, who paid the penalty for us so that we would not have to suffer eternally for the sins and mistakes we have made in the earth realm. And, we will learn through this book that He has also made a way for us to escape the earthly punishments and penalties for our wrongs and sins, known as generational and personal sin curses.

Chapter 2

Personal Sin Curses

There are two types of curses that we can experience in our lives: generational curses and personal sin curses. The primary difference between the two is this: generational curses are penalties of sins and transgressions that are judged in our children's and descendants' lives. Personal sin curses are penalties of sin and transgressions that we have committed in our lifetime, but are rather judged *during* our lifetime. In this chapter I want to deal with personal sin curses.

When I was a child, just about all the movies that were shown at that time depicted the good guys triumphing, and the bad guys either getting caught and put in jail or killed at the end of the movie. However, the late 70's and 80's began a different trend. More and more movies began to glamorize sin and lawlessness, and ended with the bad guys getting away with the crime or sin, never getting caught by the good guys or judged by God, and living life happily ever after.

But that's Hollywood. In real life there are always consequences to our continual, deliberate rebellion against God, His ways and His Word. As a child, I was constantly taught the golden rule by my mother, which was to *do to others as I wanted people to do to me.* In Galatians 6:7, the Bible tells us what happens to us if we do not treat people fairly. It says, *"you will reap what you sow."* When you do right, right and good will come back to you. But when you do wrong, and do people wrong, then wrong will also come back to you. It took me until well in my adulthood to learn this valuable life lesson. Some people never learn it and still never get the message. They never learn it because they never connect the dots of the problems, troubles and difficulties they experience later in life to the sin, transgressions and wrongdoings they dished out earlier in their life.

In 2 Samuel chapter 11 is the familiar story of David and Bathsheba. Everyone knows the story of how David became so blinded with infatuated lust for Bathsheba, that he blatantly ignored the laws of God and committed adultery, even though he knew that it was wrong. He compounded this sin even further by committing murder in an attempt to cover up his adultery.

After God confronted David through the prophet Nathan, David began to repent unto the Lord for his sins. In fact, Psalm 51 is the repentance prayer that David prayed in response to his sin. Through this Psalm you can see David's sincere heart of remorse and repentance to God for what he had done. But even though David repented greatly for his sins, he still had to pay a heavy penalty. Even though God forgave David of the eternal judgment and penalty, he still had to be judged in the physical earth realm during his lifetime for his sins.

I wanted to bring this point out because of the mistaken belief that if we confess our sins, then God forgives us and wipes the slate clean. He does in fact do this spiritually.

When we repent, all our sins are applied to the penalty Jesus paid on the cross. However, the physical, earthly penalty still has to be paid.

Again, even though David repented sorely from his heart of his adultery and murder, he still had to pay a heavy earthly penalty for these sins. First, his first son by Bathsheba died a few days after birth. Next, after David had many children by different wives, chaos broke out among them. One of his sons by the name of Amnon raped his half sister. Another son by the name of Absalom, killed his half brother, Amnon, who was the one that raped his sister, Tamar. Later, Absalom rebelled against David. In this revolt, Absalom actually overthrew the kingdom for a short while and sent David running for his life in the wilderness once again. And, finally, his son, Absalom, who was so dear to David's heart, was killed in his attempt to overthrow the kingdom.

God truly loved David. He also forgave David of his sins eternally. But yet in spite of David's sincere and heartfelt repentance, he still had to pay an earthly penalty for his sins. All these tragedies were just penalties for David's sins. They were personal sin curses. Again, personal sin curses are the earthly penalties we pay during our lifetime for sins we commit.

It Came Back Different

Many times, personal sin curses are imputed in the same manner in which they were committed. The person who cheats and steals, later has to deal with someone cheating and stealing from them. The person who becomes a liar has to deal with people they trust lying to them. This can apply to any area of life. However, personal sin curses and generational curses can many times be imputed in a totally different manner than the way they were committed.

I met a particular brother at a church conference and we managed to continue to stay in contact for awhile. One day I received a surprising phone call from him asking for prayer, telling me that he had been falsely accused of a crime. He felt that he was innocent of the crime and would be easily vindicated in court. However, things had not quite gone the way he and his lawyer had expected. He told me that his pride kept him from telling me about this problem before now. But by the time he called me, he had been tried, convicted, and was told to report to jail in a few days. He wanted me to pray that the person who falsely accused him of this crime would come forward and tell the truth and exonerate him.

As I began to pray for him, God spoke to my heart to ask him if there were something he had been doing that he knew displeased God. That's when he began to confess to me some things he had done. He was married and had a great wife. However, he was unfaithful to her for many years. Because of his business, he traveled extensively and was gone from home as much as he was there. This allowed him to establish long-term relationships with other women. For one short period of time he even committed bigamy. As he was telling me this story, I stood in shock, not believing that this was the same person I had known all this time.

The Lord revealed to me that the prison sentence he had received was not for the crime for which he was being accused, but rather the penalty of a personal sin curse for the sins he had committed earlier against God, and against his wife and family. However, the more I explained it, the less he understood it. He couldn't connect the dots because he kept focusing on the fact that he was innocent of *this* crime.

He also couldn't understand it because prior to meeting him, he said that he had stopped doing those things, asked the Lord to forgive him, and rededicated his life to the Lord. He couldn't understand the Lord allowing this to happen to him long after he had confessed his sins and asked the Lord to forgive him for them. I then explained to him that if we confess our sins, God forgives us of the eternal penalty of our sins, but there are times that He still requires an earthly penalty to also be paid.

I gave this story to illustrate the point that personal sin curses, as well as generational curses are not always imputed in the same manner in which they were committed. They are sometimes manifested in an entirely different manner. The person who lives a life of committing adultery may not necessarily have someone to commit adultery on them; they may have someone to steal from them. The person who spends their life using and abusing others may receive their payback in the form of financial struggles, problems with the law, or a host of other difficulties and struggles in life. The point is that regardless of the way in which sins are committed, the payback for those sins can come in a completely different manner. So before you begin blaming the devil for troubles, tests and trials in your life, do like David and seek the Lord as to the source of your troubles. It may not be the devil at all. It could be that judgment is being handed down to you in the form of a personal sin or generational curse.

THE CHASTENING OF THE LORD
"Why God Judges Us So Harshly"

Some may ask, why does it seem that God judges some so harshly, while others seem to get away with so much? As we look at the life of David, the same question could be asked. Why was it that Saul, who was so rebellious against God, didn't seem to get judged harshly by God at all — at least not until his death. But yet it seems that every time David stepped across the line, God judged him harshly.

I have seen this at times in my own personal life. I have known people who were cruel, heartless, ruthless, and totally ungodly, and it seems that nothing bad ever happened to them. But yet it seems that when I sneezed wrong, God judged me. This baffled me most of my life until a few years ago when God revealed to me the reason. The answer is found in the following passage:

> *...My son, despise not thou the chastening of the Lord, nor faint when thou art rebuked of him: For whom the Lord loveth he chasteneth, and scourgeth every son whom he receiveth. If ye endure chastening, God dealeth with you as with sons; for what son is he whom the father chasteneth not? But if ye be without chastisement, whereof all are partakers, then are ye bastards, and not sons.*
>
> *Hebrews 12:5-8*

The personal sin curses we pay are not sent by the devil, they are sent by God. Because God loves us, He chastens us to get us to repent and change. I was once in a workplace setting where people were discussing corporal punishment with children. They were discussing it from a secular, modern day philosophy of how cruel and inhuman it is to spank children.

After listening to this secularism for a while, I stepped in the conversation and asked this question: did your parents spank you when you were children? Each one answered, yes, along with their continued gripe about how cruel it was. My second question was this: do you think your parents spanked you just to punish you, or because they loved you and wanted to teach you to do right? They continued to hesitantly answer the question, realizing by now they were being set up.

My third question was this: did the spankings help you? Again, they answered, yes, as their facial expressions began to change. I then began to give insight into my childhood about how I thanked my mother after I became an adult for spanking me when I was a child. I explained to them that it was those spankings that kept me from sin, rebellion against God, and even crimes against man. I further explained that if it were not for those spankings I received, I probably would have ended up in jail. My last question was this: if you feel that the spankings effectively helped you, and were done out of a demonstration of love, then why don't you show your children the same kind of love? After that question, they all just sat there in amazement and couldn't say anything.

Incidentally, I'm definitely not an advocate of child abuse. Sometimes a punishment of no television or video games may be enough to change a child. But there are times, situations and incidents that warrant a spanking. Furthermore, God endorses spankings all through His Word. And, I think He knows more about the nature and soul of a child, and how to raise a child and bring proper, "effective" correction than we do.

Now, back to the subject of why God chastens us. The chastening of the Lord is actually a spiritual spanking, and God (spiritually) spanks us for the same reason we spank our children. First, He does it because He loves us, and does not want to see us fall further and further into sin and receive more of His wrath. Secondly, God would much rather judge us now in this lifetime and see us change, than allow us to continue down the road of sin and rebellion against Him and have to judge us in the life hereafter. Thirdly, like it did David, His chastening (personal sin curses) leads us back to repentance and change.

The other question I had was this: why does it seem that God deals with us more than He deals with sinners and people who don't even acknowledge Him? To answer this question, let me give you an example. Let's say that you had two young children who were having a slumber party. Along with your two children, lets say that there were five or six other children from throughout the neighborhood attending. Sometime during the evening you decided to go in their room and check on them, and surprisingly found all of them attempting to smoke cigarettes—something you had strongly cautioned your children against on many occasions. What would you do? Most parents would probably send the neighbors' kids home immediately and call their parents and tell them what happened. As for your own children, you would either spank them or find some other way to punish or discipline them. The question that now arises is this: Why wouldn't you discipline or punish the neighbors' kids who did the same thing? The answer is simple: they are not your children.

The reason you would deal with your children is because first of all, they are *your* children, and you love them and want to make sure that you train them as best as you can. And the chastisement they receive from you now as a child may keep them from having to suffer troubles and hardships later in life. In this example, a spanking may keep them from a life of cigarette addiction.

God does the same thing with His children. First, He does it because we are His own. Spiritually, there are only two fathers (God and Satan). We are born into this world with Satan as our spiritual father. But when we become born-again, we become adopted into the family of God and become the (spiritual) children of God. The second reason He chastens us is because He loves us. The closer you get to God, the closer He gets to you. I know that God loves us all, but the more we fall in love with Him, the more he loves and cherishes us.

Because He loves and cherishes us so much, He does not want to see us experience His wrath. So to keep us from His wrath, He judges us quickly to keep us from falling deeper into sin, and thereby deeper into His wrath. He loves us and wants to see us grow spiritually in His will and obedience to His Word, rather than face Him in eternal judgment—being sentenced to hell.

The closer you are to God, the more He will judge you for even the smallest sin or disobedience. But this is a good thing. I always tell our members that when God chastens you, it means that you are in the right place with God. Again, God says He loves those whom He chastens. The problem occurs when you can sin against God and there is no chastening. It's then that you are in serious trouble, and may not be walking in the love of God.

The purpose of spanking a child is not to punish them. It's to teach them to do right, and serve as a reminder of the negative consequences for disobedience. The rules parents set for their children are never meant to harm them, but rather, to help them. Once they cross those rules and receive correction for their disobedience, it serves as a constant reminder for them each time they are tempted to do that particular act again. When a child reaches up to touch a hot stove, the mother spanks the child's hand. This is not meant to abuse the child, but to help them by serving as a reminder not to touch the hot stove and possibly burn their hand.

It's the same way with God. God allows personal sin curses to come upon our lives to serve as a reminder that there are negative consequences to negative actions of sin, transgressions and disobedience. They are meant to teach us to obey God and do good. The more we learn this lesson, the more it will keep us from (burning our hand on the hot stove) the judgment hand of God.

———— Chapter 3 ————

The Famine

> *Then there was a famine in the days of David three years, year after year...*
>
> 2 Samuel 21:1

This passage is one of the foundational passages which we will use throughout this book. It begins with David and the Israelites experiencing a famine for three years in a row. A famine is a time when nothing grows upon the land. As a result of nothing growing, animals die, and the people go hungry, starve, and also may die. As we will discover, David and the Israelites experienced this famine because of a generational curse.

We can also experience spiritual famines because of generational curses. A spiritual famine is when nothing seems to grow, increase or progress in our lives or families in a particular area. We can experience a famine in our health where we are hit with sickness and disease and do not receive our healing. We can experience a famine in our finances where it seems we just continue to struggle financially over and over again. And we can also experience famines in our jobs, where we cannot seem to either find a job, keep a job, or get a promotion on our job. These are just a few of the different types of famines that can hit our lives. They can literally hit us in any area of life.

Never Assume that it's a Curse

Before we get deeper into generational curses, let me give this caution: if you are experiencing a famine in your life, do not automatically assume that it is because of a generational curse. It could be that something in your life simply needs to change. Since the revelation of generational curses became widely known in the body of Christ, people have begun to blame most of their problems and issues in life on generational curses.

Many of the problems we experience in life are not a result of generational curses. Some are simply a result of making poor choices and decisions. For example: some of our physical health problems may be as a result of a poor lifestyle, diet, eating habits, or neglect. Some of our employment problems may be due to poor work performance, punctuality and work ethics. Some of our lifelong financial problems may be due to undisciplined spending and poor financial planning.

So before you begin to assume that your problem is a generational curse, carefully examine your actions and see if there is something you could do differently. Try getting some professional help or counseling in that area such as a dietitian, financial planner, or whatever profession that deals with your situation first. Many times we will find that if we simply get the proper help or counseling and apply it to our lives, we can change our circumstances.

Generational Traits

Many people also mistakenly view their problems as generational curses when they are not generational curses at all, but rather, generational traits. There is a difference between generational curses and generational traits. Generational curses are spiritual penalties that were not paid by the culprit or originator of the sin, but are passed down to their descendants to pay. Generational traits are not necessarily spiritual, as much as they are parentally influenced.

Generational traits are characteristics or behavior that are learned or adapted by children from their parents. No one can form or influence a child's life like a parent. Because children idolize their parents, any behavior they see their parents portray—positive or negative, can easily become accepted and adopted by them. A parent can influence a child's life by the words they speak to them as well as the life they live before them. This is why it is so important for us to set good examples for our children with our lives, conversation and mannerisms, because as they grow older, they will either intentionally or unintentionally emulate what they see in us.

Social Traits

In addition to generational traits, you also have "social traits." These traits do not come from parents; they are adopted from people in their surroundings. These traits are adopted from members in their immediate family, extended family, school, neighborhood and community.

In addition to their family and community, social traits can come from friends, peers and acquaintances. They can also come from television and movies. Many parents become frustrated because they try their best to teach and train their children to do right, and to have the right ethics, moral fiber and character in life. But because of the negative influences of their friends and peers, as well as a strong ungodly media influence, children's character is many times influenced and swayed more toward the negative influences around them, than the good influences from their parents and other positive role models.

Generational and social traits can easily be misconstrued and misunderstood as generational curses because of the similarity in the way they are passed down from one generation to another. You may have seen families that continue to experience the same cycle of negative and adverse behavior generation after generation. Instead of it being generational, it's quite possible that each generation has simply accepted and adopted the adverse behavior from their surroundings and continue to pass it down to each generation.

The generational and social traits are adapted lifestyles, while the generational curses are spiritually inherited. When a generational curse is upon a person, no matter what you change in their life, they are going to always fall back to the same cycle or pattern. But generational and social traits can be corrected with teaching, counseling, hard work, or a change in their surroundings.

I once saw a movie in the 80's that was a good portrayal of a generational or social trait. It was a movie entitled, *Trading Places*. It depicted the star, Eddie Murphy, as a poor, peddling, swindling street thug. He was taken out of the environment in which he was raised and put into a positive, affluent environment where he was trained and schooled. His new environment now caused him to change. He no longer wanted to be a low-life scoundrel anymore. His character was now changed, and he wanted to stay that way. But if a person is under a generational curse, it wouldn't matter how much they changed their atmosphere, environment or surroundings, they would continue to fall back to the same lifestyle until the spirit and curse were broken.

The Redundant Famine

Then there was a famine in the days of David three years, year after year...
2 Samuel 21:1

Again, David and the Israelites experienced this famine over and over again. I'm sure that after David had the first year of famine, he probably told the farmers to use better fertilizer the next year. After the second year of famine he probably told them to use more seed. But by the third year of famine, David realized that this problem had nothing to do with the farmers' fertilizer, seeds, or efforts, but rather, a spiritual problem instead.

We said earlier that before you assume that a problem you may be experiencing is a curse, make sure you have done everything you can to change your circumstances. If necessary, you must be willing to make changes, get professional help and counseling, and be willing to both receive and apply the information you obtain to your life. Until you have effectively sought help for your situation, received it, and applied it to your life, do not assume that it is a curse.

David (assumingly) did everything under his power to change their circumstances (the famine), but kept getting the same results over and over again. One of the ways you can know that you are in a famine (that is a curse) is when you have likewise done everything in your power to change your circumstances, and yet no matter how hard you try, how much you work, or how much effort you put forth to change it, nothing seems to work. If you have truly done everything you can, and you or your family seem to continue to experience the same issues over and over again, it could be that you are under a curse and need God's deliverance.

No Way Out

> *And the king called the Gibeonites, and said unto them... what shall I do for you? and wherewith shall I make the atonement, that ye may bless the inheritance of the LORD?* <u>*And the Gibeonites said unto him, We will have no silver nor gold of Saul, nor of his house; neither for us shalt thou kill any man in Israel....*</u>
>
> 2 Samuel 21:2-4

After David sought the face of God, the Lord revealed to him that this was a generational curse that was placed upon them because of the sins of Saul. David then called the Gibeonites and asked them what he could do in order for them to release he and the Israelites from this generational curse.

Their response began with them stating that they didn't want any amount of money nor anything else from David and the Israelites. This represents the fact that when there's a personal or generational curse upon your life or family (until it is broken), there is nothing you can physically do (on your own without God's intervention) to break it until the time and penalty has been fulfilled.

We said earlier that when the famine hit David and the Israelites, they probably did all they could do to change the course of this famine. But no matter what they did, the famine continued. Likewise, when there is a personal or generational curse upon our lives, there is nothing we can do to stop or abort it without the help and deliverance of the Lord. Again, it doesn't matter how hard you work, how well you plan, how well you prepare, or how much knowledge you obtain and apply to your life; the same things will continue to happen over and over again until the established time and penalties have been fulfilled or the curse is broken.

There is no pattern of specifics for a generational curse. The length of time, severity, and type of generational curse varies. Some generational curses are more specific to a particular family. Some are reserved for a specific gender in a family.

Seek The Face of the Lord

Then there was a famine in the days of David three years, year after year; <u>and David inquired of the LORD</u>....

2 Samuel 21:1

We said earlier that before you assume that you are under a curse, you need to do like David and do everything you can to overcome the obstacle. After you have made changes, sought help, and still continue to experience the same recurring results, the next thing you must do is to do like David and *"inquire of the Lord."* This is simply to make sure you honestly seek the face of the Lord.

The reason why I emphasize "honestly" seek God is because many people pray to God, but are not open to the truth about their lives or circumstances. In John 8:32, Jesus said, **"And ye shall know the truth, and the truth shall make you free."** If we are going to get set free or receive God's deliverance in our lives, we must also be willing to receive the truth about ourselves. In Proverbs 12:15, it says that every man feels that he is right in his own eyes. What is so deceiving is that some people feel that they are right in their own eyes to the point that no one can tell them anything. Some will not receive the truth from their friends, family, spouse, or even their pastor. And, many are so self-deceived that even though they pray to God, they are still not open and willing to receive the truth about themselves even from God. This is the reason why God said in Isaiah 1:19 that it's only when we are *"willing and obedient"* that we will *eat the fruit of the land* (receive His blessings and deliverance). To be willing and obedient is to be open and willing to receive the counsel of the Holy Spirit and obey the counsel you receive from Him.

The reason why people have a problem receiving the truth from the Spirit of God is because of Satan, the mind blinder. Satan blinds the person from the truth to the point that they are spiritually blinded, and cannot see or recognize the truth about themselves. Although they can easily see and recognize the truth in the lives of everyone else around them, they are blinded to seeing or recognizing the truth about their lives (even from God). And, until they both recognize, and are willing to receive the truth about themselves, they will continue to suffer and pay the penalties of personal and generational curses, as well as other pitfalls and setbacks in their lives.

So if there is a recurring famine in your life or family, the first thing you need to do is pray and ask the Lord to help you to be open and willing to not only hear the truth, but to also be open to receive the truth—even if it hurts. You then do like David did and pray and ask Him to reveal to you if you are truly under a curse; and if you are, the nature or source of the curse.

You must be serious about hearing Him speak to you. After you pray and seek Him, be (like Daniel) willing to faithfully, patiently and diligently wait for the answer. You may or may not get a quick, microwave response from the Lord. Sometimes it may require hours, days or even weeks of praying and seeking the Lord for your answer. It may even require you to do like Daniel and fast to get the answer from the Lord. You must truly want His truth, pray for His truth, and be willing to do whatever He requires of you to get His truth. And, when you come to the Lord with this type of humility, persistence and determination, like He did with David, He will answer you. And when you apply His truths through His principles and precepts, the truth that you both receive and apply will truly set you free.

―――― Chapter 4 ――――

The History

HISTORY OF THE GIBEONITES
"The Covenant With the Gibeonites"

Then there was a famine in the days of David three years, year after year; and David inquired of the LORD. And the LORD answered, it is for Saul, and for his bloody house, because he slew <u>the Gibeonites</u>.

2 Samuel 21:1

After David tried everything in his power to avert the famine, he finally decided to seek the face of the Lord for the answer as to why he was having this recurring problem. God then gave David the reason for this curse. It was because of what Saul had done to the Gibeonites. But in order to understand the significance of God's answer to David, I need to go back and give you a little historical background on what happened with the Gibeonites.

The book of Joshua begins with the account of the children of Israel's invasion of the Promised Land under Joshua's regime. This took place 40 years after Moses' generation failed to take the land because of their sins, lack of faith, and their fear. God told Joshua and the Israelites to go over and take everything. After they had successfully taken Jericho and the next city of Ai, they were on their way to their third conquest, which was supposed to be the city of Gibeon. But the people of Gibeon had heard of the great and mighty exploits of God through the Israelites.

They had heard of the miracles in Egypt, and how God delivered them from Pharaoh and Egypt (the world power of that time). They heard how God had parted the Red Sea and brought them across on dry land; they heard how He had provided for them for 40 years in the desert wilderness. They had also heard about the miraculous miracle at Jericho, and their victory over the capital city of Ai.

They knew that there was no possible way whatsoever they could defeat this nation with God behind them, so they resulted to trickery. They sent ambassadors to intercept Joshua and the Israelites about a three-day's journey before they would have reached Gibeon. They deceptively disguised these ambassadors to look as though they had been traveling for months. They had molded bread, wineskins that were busted and worn, shoes that had holes in them, and their clothes were worn and torn.

The ambassadors told Joshua that they were from a distant continent, and had been traveling for months. They also told Joshua that they had heard about the greatness of their God, and wanted to make a covenant with them to serve their God. They asked Joshua and the Israelites to make a covenant with them; they also promised that with this covenant, they would both serve them and pay them taxes.

Since Joshua was under the supposition they were not part of the Promised Land, they considered this proposal from the Gibeonites to be an unexpected extra blessing. So without seeking God, they went ahead and made the covenant with them and continued on their way.

After a three-day's journey to their next conquest, guess who they run into—The Gibeonites. Even though they tricked Joshua and the Israelites into making a covenant not to destroy them, because the covenant was made in the sight of God, they had to honor their covenant and could not harm them. So the Gibeonites became their servants and were allowed to live among them in the land.

Saul Destroys The Gibeonites

...And David inquired of the LORD. And the LORD answered, it is for Saul, and for his bloody house, <u>because he slew the Gibeonites</u>.
2 Samuel 21:1

Generations later, Saul becomes king. By this time the Gibeonites had been living among the Israelites for many years. They served them and paid the Israelites taxes. One day while Saul was in one of his rages, he decided that the Gibeonites should not be allowed to live among them, and went on a rampage killing hundreds of them. This became a great sin because of the covenant that Joshua and the Israelites had made before God generations earlier not to harm them.

A generation later, Saul is now dead and David becomes the king. At that time David was living comfortably in his new position with all going well for him and the kingdom. Then all of a sudden a devastating famine broke out three years in a row. After David finally sought the Lord as to the cause of the famine after the third year, God revealed to David that this was a curse that was placed upon the Israelites because of the sins of Saul a generation earlier. Even though Saul was now dead, God was judging the Israelites for something that Saul's generation had done.

Judgment Upon Another Generation

We have discovered that there are two penalties that must be paid for our sins: the physical in this lifetime, and the spiritual in the hereafter. In Matthew 6:12, Jesus taught us to pray that God would forgive us of our "debts." Another translation calls them trespasses. Whenever we sin against God, we trespass or violate His law. Whenever we violate God's laws, someone has to pay the penalty.

In breaking some of our mild laws such as receiving a speeding violation, we can actually call someone on the phone, and they can come to the police station and pay our fine for us.

Spiritually speaking, we can commit violations against God in our lifetime, and someone else can also (involuntarily) pay our penalty. Our eternal penalty was paid by our Lord, Jesus Christ, when he died on the cross. Those of us who accept Him and receive Him into our hearts will go to heaven because Jesus paid the penalty for us with His suffering on the cross. Before He died on the cross, He said, "It is finished." He said this meaning that the eternal penalty (wages) for all of our sins, transgressions and iniquities had been fully paid and completed.

However, as we discovered earlier, there is still a physical, earthly penalty that must be paid. Now if we repent, God will sometimes not judge us for the sins and transgressions we commit. God did not judge David and the Israelites for every sin Saul had committed, but there were some, and this just happened to be one of them.

The judgment or consequences of these sins are sometimes passed down to other generations. Just as in the above incident with David and the Gibeonites, sometimes God judges a generation for sins and transgressions that were committed by their parents and ancestors. The judgment of these sins upon another generation is called a generational curse.

The Essentials of Family History

Now that we understand the history of what happened with Saul and the Gibeonites, we can now understand more about the curse that came upon David and the Israelites. Likewise, it is also important for us to learn and understand the history of our ancestors. Just as David's predecessor caused their generation to suffer this curse, our predecessors (parents and other ancestors) can also be the cause of some of our curses.

When you go to a new doctor, one of the first things the receptionist does is to ask you to fill out a family history questionnaire for the doctor. They want you to provide your family history as far back as you are aware. This family history helps to give the doctor an idea of your susceptibility to certain illnesses and diseases.

In the same manner, it is a good idea (if possible) to also get a family history of some of the negative issues and problems in your family. Most of the time we like to only think the best of our parents. If you had a good mother or father, it is very hard to imagine them doing anything sinful. We often conjure up fairytale, *"Mary Poppins"* visualizations of our mother, and *"Father Knows Best"* visualizations of our father. And if anybody says anything contrary to our fantasy visualization of them that we have created in our minds, we are ready to *"lay our religion down"* and *"get ready to rumble."*

When you go to the doctor, you know that the information you give him will help him to better treat you. So you then become honest with him and truthfully give him the information on every illness, disease, and problem that you are aware of in your family's history to the best of your knowledge.

If you are going to get help and deliverance from your generational curses, you are going to have to likewise get honest with yourself, come out of Disneyland, and take a clear objective look at *"The Good, The Bad, and The Ugly"* issues in the lives of your parents, grandparents, and other ancestors.

Papa Was a Rolling Stone

When I was a teenager, a song came out by a group called the *Temptations,* entitled, *"Papa Was a Rolling Stone."* It describes the story of children whose father had just died. The children had heard many negative things about their father throughout the years, and now wanted to know the truth from their mother. The mother finally sat her children down and opened up and honestly told them the truth about their father. In the song, *"Papa"* had a lot of bad attributes. It describes him as a man who was lazy and never kept a steady job, an adulterer, bigamist, hypocrite, drunkard, and several other bad attributes.

In the song, the children wanted to know the truth about their father. Fictionally, knowing the truth about *Papa* in the song could have possibly helped the children to better understand some things about themselves. Likewise, knowing the truth about our parents, grandparents, uncles, aunts and others in our family tree and family line may help us to better understand some of the struggles and temptations in our own lives.

I'm not saying that you need to necessarily go around asking for negative information regarding your parents and ancestors, but at the same time, you should also be careful not to ignorantly ignore the truth of what you have both seen and heard about their lives.

In 1 Peter 4:8, it says, "*love covers a multitude of faults.*" My mother loved my siblings and me, and did all she could to show each of us her love, and raise us the best she could. And, even though through the years I came to see and learn a few negative things about my mother's life, because of the love she had for us, and the love I had for her, it never damaged or even tarnished my ideology or perception of her at all. If your parents love you and you love them, I'm sure that the negative things you may have seen or heard about them will likewise not tarnish the love, honor and respect you have for them.

Take a Close Look

Learning some things about my parents' and grandparents' lives through the years, along with seeing some things in the lives of my older siblings and other close relatives helped me to identify some areas of my life where there may have been some generational curses. As I have been able to identify and aggressively deal with them through the points and precepts of this book, I have been able to overcome and destroy just about all of them.

If you have seen some negative things recur throughout your family's genealogy, it could be that your family is under a curse and needs God's deliverance.

If you are contemplating marriage, or if you are a parent whose child is contemplating marriage, be very observant of the person's family. The engagement period is not merely a time to simply play like you're married; it's a time to also carefully examine both your fiancé and their family to see if they are what they appear to be.

They are probably not going to willingly divulge anything negative about their lives, siblings' lives, or their parents. But as you pray and ask God to reveal the truth to you about them, He will reveal things to you. Pay very careful attention to traits and characteristics in the lives of their parents and siblings. Spend time getting to know them also. Recurring traits in the lives of their siblings could be a sign that there is some type of generational curse involved.

You need to know this because you need to make a wise, prayerful decision of whether or not to go into the marriage. And, if you do decide to go into it, at least you will know what you (and possibly later on, your children) will be dealing with.

Chapter 5

Inherited Judgment

Now that we understand the history of why Saul's attack on the Gibeonites brought this curse upon David and the Israelites, we now want to explore how and why the sinful and negative actions of one generation are passed down as a penalty and a curse to another generation.

THE SUBSTITUTE JUDGMENT

> *And they answered the king, The man that consumed us, and that devised against us that we should be destroyed from remaining in any of the coasts of Israel, let seven men of his sons be delivered unto us, and we will hang them up unto the LORD in Gibeah of Saul, whom the LORD did choose. And the king said, I will give them.*
> —2 Samuel 21:5-6

After God revealed to David that they were under a generational curse because of what Saul had done to the Gibeonites, David went to inquire of them what they needed to do to get released from the curse. The Gibeonites' answer to David was that they wanted him to give them seven sons of Saul to hang for the revenge of Saul ordering the slaughter of so many of their people.

To understand the Bible, especially the Old Testament, you must first understand the "Law of Representation." In this Law of Representation, the Gibeonites were the ones who were offended. This offense took place in a previous generation. Just because the penalty was not carried out upon Saul during his lifetime doesn't mean that the sin or trespass must go unpunished. After Saul's death, the penalty became the responsibility of his descendants to pay. Therefore, the Gibeonites represent generational curses. When they asked for seven sons of Saul to be hung, this represents the spirit of the Gibeonites rising up and crying out to God for vengeance for the injustice done to them even long after that person is dead and gone.

In many instances in the Bible, you find God telling a person that someone's blood was crying out to Him from the grave. This cry that God refers to in His Word is the spirit of the Gibeonites that cries from the grave when a person has done evil and unjust, and the penalty was not paid by the culprit during their natural, physical life. It's a constant cry for justice, vengeance and judgment. The spirit of the Gibeonites also cries out for other gross types of sin and unrighteousness that goes unpunished and unjudged during the person's earthly, physical life.

Again, even though the person who committed the sins or transgressions may be dead and long gone, the penalty still can be paid. It's paid by the (sons) descendants.

Although King Saul began as a good king, he changed and disobeyed God and turned into an evil, unrighteous king. Saul was not judged physically during his lifetime for this sin against the Gibeonites. Therefore when the Gibeonites had a chance to ask for vengeance, they demanded the next best thing—seven of his sons. These seven sons of Saul became a "substitute" for Saul.

The sons of Saul therefore represent the "Substitute Judgment." The "Substitute Judgment" means that the person or people who committed a crime, transgression or offense is not alive, so the spirit of the Gibeonites cries out from the grave to God for a relative substitute to take their punishment. This is what happened with the case of David. Since Saul was now dead, seven of his sons were requested for a comparable, relative substitute.

The same thing holds true to our day. It could be that someone has done evil generations earlier, and they are now dead and gone. But the spirit of the Gibeonites can still come up to cry to God for vengeance and justice for the sin, transgression or injustice that was committed and went unpaid. Because the originator of the sin becomes deceased, it does not stop the cry of the spirit of the Gibeonites. Because if the originator is dead, the spirit of the Gibeonites asks for the penalty to be carried out on the next best thing—a living relative or family member to serve as a substitute for the judgment.

The Law of Inherited Debt

An example of substitute judgment can be found in the story of the widow woman and the pot of oil in 2 Kings chapter 4. This widow woman's husband was a servant of God who served faithfully but was now dead. But in those days, if someone died owing money to a creditor, the children then became responsible for paying the debt. If they couldn't pay the debt, the creditor would have the right to either put them in jail, or make them their servants until the debt was paid.

In this story, the father died still owing the creditors. Neither the wife nor children had anything to pay the creditors. The creditors were now on their way to put the woman's two sons in jail and make them slaves until the debt was paid off. Even though they had nothing to do with making the loan, the children were still responsible for paying it off because the creditors could legally make the children the substitute for the loan.

You know the rest of the story. God used Elisha to perform the miracle of the oil. The woman only had one pot of oil. God multiplied the oil over and over again—filling up her entire house with oil. She then went into the oil business and sold the oil, making enough money to pay the creditors off and still live off the rest, thus keeping her sons from being put in jail and becoming slaves.

In this story, the reason the creditors could make the children responsible for the debt of their deceased father was because of the law of "Inherited Debt." This is a law that no longer exists in our society. In our society, once a person dies, the only thing that a creditor can make a stake or claim on is the property and assets once owned by the deceased.

In the law of inherited debt that existed in those days, just as children could inherit property and assets from their deceased parents, they also inherited the responsibility of their deceased parents' debt. And, if they were unable to pay their creditors, they could be placed in jail or placed into servitude until the debt was fully paid.

Even though we no longer have the law of inherited debt in our society, it still exists spiritually. Generational curses operate under this form of substitute judgment with the law of inherited debt. Just as the sons of this widow woman inherited the debt responsibility of their father (even though he was dead), spiritually, we can also inherit (unpaid) debts of our ancestors. The generational curses are the payment for the (debts) sins.

Many times the sins a person commits in life is also paid by them later in life in the form of personal sin curses. But there are some debts that go unpunished in a person's physical life. They die without paying their physical debt for that sin. That debt is then carried over to their descendants to pay the debt in the same manner in which the widow woman's children became responsible for their father's debt after he had passed.

Again, not all of the sins of the parents become the responsibility of their descendants to pay. We stated earlier that Saul had a life of lawlessness and disobedience, but David only became responsible for this one sin. No one knows what sins for which the spirit of the Gibeonites will begin to cry about to God for vengeance and justice. Neither does anyone know *when* they will rise and cry. But when they do, and God grants it, someone will have to pay.

Chapter 6

Inherited Giants

SONS OF THE GIANT

> *Moreover the Philistines had yet war again with Israel; and David went down, and his servants with him, and fought against the Philistines: and David waxed faint. And Ishbibenob, which was of the sons of the giant, the weight of whose spear weighed three hundred shekels of brass in weight, he being girded with a new sword, thought to have slain David. But Abishai the son of Zeruiah succoured him, and smote the Philistine, and killed him.*
>
> 2 Samuel 21:15-17

In this passage David was in war once again. During the battle, David became exhausted and weak, and a giant (one of the sons of the giant Goliath) cornered David and was about to kill him. But one of David's men by the name of Abishai came to David's rescue and killed the giant.

To understand the significance of this passage you have to go back to the story of David and Goliath. Saul was king at that time, and David was about twelve years old. The war was the responsibility of King Saul. After David's conquest and victory over Goliath, the Israelites pursued the Philistines only a short while. King Saul was satisfied with obtaining this mighty victory and did not fully pursue the Philistines. But in the complacency of this victory, he failed to address the fact that Goliath also had a brother and three sons—all of which were giants. He should have not only killed Goliath; he should have also sought after and killed Goliath's brother and his sons.

> *And it came to pass after this, that there was again a battle with the Philistines at Gob: then Sibbechai the Hushathite slew Saph, which was of the <u>sons of the giant</u>. And there was again a battle in Gob with the Philistines, where Elhanan the son of Jaareoregim, a Bethlehemite, slew the <u>brother of Goliath</u> the Gittite, the staff of whose spear was like a weaver's beam. And there was yet a battle in Gath, where was a man of great stature, that had on every hand six fingers, and on every foot six toes, four and twenty in number; and he also was <u>born to the giant</u>. And when he defied Israel, Jonathan the son of Shimeah the brother of David slew him. These four were born to the giant in Gath, and fell by the hand of David, and by the hand of his servants.* —2 Samuel 21:18-22

The above two passages tell us of four giants that became a serious threat to David and the Israelites. Goliath and his brothers represent sinful and ungodly strongholds that we allow to become developed in our lives. They become developed in our lives the same reason that Saul did not kill Goliath's brother and sons—complacency.

When God told Joshua and the Israelites to take the promised land, He told them to go in and destroy all—men, women and children. In our modern day conventional wars this might seem barbaric. But there was a reason why God told them to do it. It's because of what they represent.

The Men: They represent the obvious problem. Let's use someone with a smoking habit for an example. The men represent the cigarettes. Some would think that the cigarettes are the problem for someone with a smoking addiction. Therefore they make a feeble attempt to throw the cigarettes away—thinking that this would solve the problem of smoking—but it doesn't. I once saw a commercial advertising a cigarette patch, where a man attempted to quit smoking by throwing his cigarettes in the garbage. The next day you find the man digging through the garbage to retrieve the cigarettes he threw away the day before.

The Women and Children: They represent the spirit behind the problem. The reason the man went back in the garbage to retrieve the cigarettes is because he did not deal with the women and children—the spirit behind the problem or addiction. Throwing away the cigarettes is only a short-term solution. You have to also get to the source of the addiction (the spirit behind it). Once you deal with the spirit behind the problem, you can then throw away the cigarettes for good. This is the reason why God had them to kill everyone in the land. It symbolized for us the need to get rid of the spirit along with the problem.

What Satan desires in our lives is to get a toehold, then a foothold, and eventually a stronghold:

A Toehold would be described as a small sin that is occasionally committed.

A Foothold is a problem, sin or habit that becomes larger. It is no longer an occasional sin or transgression. It has now become moderately frequent. The ability to resist it becomes harder and harder.

A Stronghold is a problem, sin or addiction that has become fully developed and is out of control. It is now a full-fledged habit or addiction. The ability to resist it is short-lived and often futile.

When God commanded Joshua and the Israelites to destroy the inhabitants of the land (men, women and children), the giants of the land were also included in that mix. Goliath represents the strongholds we allow to become established in our lives. It's the sin that creeps in that we refuse to deal with. It becomes stronger and bigger, until it becomes a giant (stronghold).

Many Christians secretly live with strongholds. They know they are there; but because of the spirit of compromise, they live with these sins, allowing them to grow stronger and stronger. Their only concern is that they do not get caught or exposed in them. As long as they can keep their internal struggle a secret, they are satisfied with living with them. So they compromise, allowing their secret to continue to fester. They die, never having gained victory over these strongholds, thinking that it's all over. But it's not!

Sons and Brothers of Goliath

You could describe the Philistines that the Israelites (Under King Saul) fought as toeholds and footholds. You could describe Goliath as a stronghold in a person's life. If a stronghold is not aggressively dealt with, it can lead to problems in their descendants' lives.

Because Saul failed to deal with Goliath's brother and sons, David (now a generation later) had to fight them, and was almost killed by one of them. This signifies the necessity for us to get control and deliverance of the strongholds in our lives. If you do not get control and victory over the strongholds in your life for righteousness sake, you need to get control and victory over them for the sake of your children and descendants.

Because of your complacency and failure to overcome strongholds you allow to become developed in your life, your children and descendants may have difficult, lifelong struggles with these same strongholds, which should have been fought and conquered during your life.

In verses 15-17, you find David needing the help of Abishai to deliver him from one of these giants. Had it not been for him, David would have been killed. This is symbolic to the fact that if you do not get victory over your strongholds, they are going to be carried down to your children and descendants. And just as David needed the help of Abishai to help him to overcome the physical giant, your descendants are going to need someone to help them to get deliverance from the same giants (strongholds) you should have dealt with during your life.

Inherited Spirits

Another form of generational curses is called "Inherited Spirits." When a person has allowed a stronghold to become developed in their lives, it means that a demonic spirit has managed to get a strong (stronghold) grip on their soul. Again, if they do not get control over these (stronghold) "giants," they can die and pass these same spirits down to their children. They are not passed down to the next generation through the bloodstream like AIDS; they are passed through the spirit-realm.

Again, David was almost killed by one of Goliath's sons.

We said earlier that this happened as a result of Saul's compromise and negligence in not dealing with the giants during his day. And as a result of his compromise and negligence, David had to deal with them during his day. This is a representation of how stronghold spirits are passed down from one generation to another.

Although David is known for his intimate worship and love for God, he was also known for his lust and infatuation with Bathsheba. David's lust did not end with Bathsheba. It followed him to his death. Prior to his death, David was old and could not get warm. No matter how many clothes and blankets they attempted to use to warm him, he still could not get warm. Then the king's servants came up with the ideal of getting a young beautiful virgin to lie with David. Although she did not have intimacy with David, her presence kept him warm when nothing else worked. How do you suppose the servants knew this would work? The solution did not come through a divine revelation from God. They knew it because they knew of David's younger days, and the problems he had with lust. When David died, the spirit of lust did not die with him. It was inherited by two of his sons.

Amnon's Inherited Rage of Lust

In 2 Samuel chapter 13, Amnon, one of David's sons thought he was in love with his half-sister, by the name of Tamar. I used the phrase "thought he was in love" because it wasn't true love at all. The kind of love Amnon had for Tamar was "Eros" love. Eros love is a type of pure lust that disguises itself as genuine love. From this word "Eros" is where we get our modern word, "Erotic." Erotic love is pure sexual lust of the eyes for the flesh.

Amnon was full of this type of lustful, erotic love for his own (half) sister. Through deception he managed to get her alone and asked her to have sex with him. When she refused to do it willingly, he then forcefully raped her. After he had finished, all the love he thought he had then turned to rage and hatred towards her. He then despised her and told her to get out.

Where do you suppose Amnon got this rage of lust? It was passed down to him by his father, David. When spirits are passed down, they do not necessarily hit every descendant. So every one of David's children did not inherit this rage of lust, but some did. Incidentally, Amnon's rape did not go unpunished. He was later killed by Tamar's brother, Absalom, in revenge for raping his sister.

Solomon's Inherited Rage of Lust

After David died, his son, Solomon, became king. We all know Solomon as the wisest man that ever lived. However, even though he had all this wisdom, it still did not stop him from inheriting David's spirit of lust from being passed down to him. Solomon was not only the wisest man that ever lived, he was also one of the richest that ever lived. He had an abundance of everything.

In order to fulfill his rage of lust, he kept adding more and more wives and concubines. He didn't realize that this uncontrollable, never fulfilled hunger for lust and sex was inherited from his father, David. It was not uncommon for kings to have many wives and concubines. Many kings had ten, twenty or thirty wives and concubines. But because of Solomon's lust, he had an extreme overkill. He had seven hundred wives and three hundred concubines. That is a thousand women to fulfill his lusts and erotic desires. He could literally have had a different woman every night and not touch the same woman for almost three years.

But like David's other son, Amnon, Solomon's lust led to his demise. Even though God had strictly warned Solomon not to intermingle with or marry women from other nations that did not fear God, Solomon's lust blinded his eyes to God's commandment. He blatantly disobeyed God and further fed his uncontrollable lust by marrying women from these nations—an act which was strictly forbidden by God.

In 1 Kings chapter 11, it says that Solomon loved these foreign, idol-worshiping women. But this word "love" is the same type of love David's other son, Amnon had. It was a lustful, lascivious, erotic love.

Solomon started off in the footsteps of his father David—fearing God and strictly obeying His commandments and laws. But towards the end of his life, he allowed his lusts for these idol-worshiping women to bring him down.

Solomon allowed them to build detestable demonic idols on the hilltops. He later began allowing them to freely burn incense. He even allowed them to make sacrifices to these same demonic idols. Solomon did all this even after the Lord had appeared to him twice, warning him of this. All this happened as a result of the spirit of lust that was passed down to him.

When someone inherits a spirit or stronghold from their ancestor, it can become extremely difficult to break or overcome. In fact, to the person, it can almost appear that they are possessed and have no control over the sin, habit or addiction.

Inherited Strongholds

In our society, homosexuality and lesbianism have been accepted by many as a type of birth defect. Even though the gay and lesbian community despise the term, "birth defect," they widely accept and promote its meaning. They believe that just as there are babies born with physical abnormalities, they are born with a type of sexual abnormality. I used to sternly debate the concept that anyone was born a homosexual. I still totally disagree that anyone is born as a homosexual. But as God gave me more understanding on this subject of inherited spirits, I came to find that they are somewhat, slightly, partially right.

Although they were not born as a female trapped in a male's body, or vice versa, they were born with something that influenced their way of thinking. People who have been a victim of generational inherited spirits are people who are born with certain demonic influences on their lives from birth.

When the generational inherited spirit is passed down to another generation, it is usually in the same area. However, sometimes it can become manifested in different branches of the same sin. For example, the ancestor could have developed strongholds of lust or other heterosexual sin and promiscuity. And for the first and second generation, it could have been manifested the same way. But by the time the curse is passed down three or four generations, it could branch off that sexual stronghold and become manifested in the descendants' lives in the form of homosexuality. This is why parents of homosexuals are often baffled as to where the homosexuality came from in their children since they did not have it themselves. It came from someone in their family line. It began as a heterosexual sin, but by the time it was passed down several generations, it branched off into a different sexual perversion.

Again, these stronghold inherited spirits can be so strong, that the person is convinced that they were born this way. This is why homosexuals are convinced that they were born with this type of birth abnormality. The truth is that they are not born homosexuals; they were simply born with a stronghold spirit that is attached to their soul. This demonic influence can even be manifested in men having effeminate ways and women having masculine ways.

As they grow up, they later begin to experience feelings of being attracted to the same sex. These feelings are not natural feelings; they are caused by the strong demonic influences in that area that have been passed down to them from another generation.

The next stage begins with experimentation. As they reject the warning of the Spirit of God that is imprinted on the soul of every living being of right and wrong, and yield to the sin of this act, the appetite of homosexual lust keeps getting stronger and stronger.

This continues into early adulthood. By this time, they have given up on attempting to resist this spirit and have adapted it as their lifestyle. They become totally convinced that they were born this way and there is nothing they can do about it. But what has happened is that there is such a strong demonic influence upon them in this particular area, that they cannot distinguish what is natural from what is spiritual. If a generational inherited spirit is not dealt with aggressively, and is toyed and experimented with, the stronghold can carry the same drive and addiction as a drug addict or alcoholic.

The Mind Blinder

In whom the <u>god of this world hath blinded the minds</u> of them which believe not, lest the light of the glorious gospel of Christ, who is the image of God, should shine unto them. —2 Corinthians 4:4

Once this spirit is accepted and received, it blinds the mind of the person to the truth. They exhibit the same symptoms of a person who suffers with anorexia. The anorexic person's mind is so distorted, that they see themselves as overweight, when in fact they are not overweight at all. In the same manner, the mind of the homosexual becomes so blinded by Satan and distorted to the truth, that they believe the lie from the devil that they were actually born this way.

Those who seek God's deliverance can be delivered from this spirit just as people can receive deliverance from other strongholds or addictions. But those who ignore and reject God's Word and deliverance, and yield and receive this spirit will suffer a life of bondage to this spirit in this life, and receive God's eternal wrath in the life hereafter.

I only used the plight of the homosexual as an example. So before you begin to look down at the homosexual, you need to take a good look at, and judge your own life. Because the same pattern of generational inherited spirits that I've just gone through with the homosexual is the same pattern that takes place in other more socially accepted types of generational inherited spirits.

Because society accepts a lifestyle of heterosexual sins as normal or acceptable, does not mean that God does. They are still just as destructive, and can destroy a person's life or even send them to hell just as easily. Other sexual manifestations of this spirit are strongholds of fornication, adultery, pornography and voyeurism.

* Note: To understand more about how spirits are passed on through sexual sins, please order our teaching on CD entitled, "*Fornication, Dealing with Demons.*"

Inherited spirits can also become manifested in other non-sexual manifestations. They can even be inherited in life-long health and weight issues such as gluttony, obesity, life-long weight control problems, and can even contribute to some of our modern day diseases such as diabetes, hypertension, heart disease and many others. There are a host of others that I have not even named.

When a person inherits a stronghold spirit, it does not

mean that they are helpless to the control of the influential spirit. It only means that they will have a much stronger (demonic) influence towards a particular sin than the average person, and it will be much more difficult for them to break and overcome it. But just as people can get deliverance from difficult addictions such as smoking, drugs, alcohol, overeating, obesity and other strongholds and adverse addictions, they can get deliverance from homosexuality, lesbianism, pornography, lust, or any other inherited spirit.

Incidentally, the fact that a person was born with an inherited sprit will be no excuse when they stand before God in judgment. In Isaiah 58:6, God said that He sent Jesus Christ *"to loose the bands of wickedness, to undo the heavy burdens, and to let the oppressed go free, and break every yoke!"* These four patterns of deliverance represent four types of deliverance we may need in life—one of which is inherited spirits. In 2 Samuel chapter 15 we gave the story about David fighting the giants again. In this passage we said that David was almost killed by one of the sons of Goliath, but he was helped by Abishai. He (Abishai) represents the help of the Holy Spirit that is available to us.

Like David, many of us have had to fight the brothers and sons of Goliath (inherited spirits). But just as David got help and overcame his giants, we can do the same. God has given us the help of the Holy Spirit, His anointing, and His Word. And, through the revelation of this book, as well as others that deal with this subject, He has also given us help. We can either receive His help and overcome and destroy Goliath's brothers and sons in our lives, or we can ignore His help and live a life of defeat. The spiritual Abishai is ready to come to your rescue. The real question is, are you ready and willing to receive it?

Chapter 7

Generational Blessings

Before I continue with the next topic on the source of generational curses, I want to take a moment and share a good side of receiving something from your parents and ancestors. That is, just as we can receive a generational curse to pay the penalties of our parents and ancestors, we can also receive generational blessings because of their lives of righteousness, godliness and charity.

1 Kings 11:11-13

Most who have read any of my writings see the love I had for my mother. She was a good and godly woman who taught her children honesty, integrity, how to treat people, and most importantly, how to serve the Lord with all our hearts and obey His commandments. She also tried her best to live this example before us.

There are times I have looked at my life and wondered why the Lord has been so merciful to me and blessed me so much. It's not that I was rich or had fame or fortune or something; I've just always been thankful for the little things for which God had blessed me.

As I wondered this one day, the Lord spoke to my heart and said that part of my blessings were because of my mother's life. Although she was far from perfect, God rewarded me with mercy and grace because of the godly life she lived before Him.

This was the same case in the above passage. All of us have read how that Solomon was the wisest man that ever lived. But not only was Solomon the wisest man that ever lived, he was also the richest that ever lived. But none of the riches or wisdom that Solomon received came because of his life, but because of his Father, David. It was because David served the Lord with all of his heart that God blessed Solomon to be the richest and wisest man in the world. But not only did Solomon get the blessings because of David, he also got mercy because of David.

Although Solomon began in the footsteps of his father, David—obeying God and keeping His commandments, in his old age he abandoned the ways of God. The spirit of pride filled Solomon's heart in who he was, what he had, and how wise he was, that he completely ignored and abandoned God's laws and statues. He built idols and demonic places of worship for Chemosh, the satanic god of the Moabites, Molech, the satanic god of the Ammonites, and Ashteroth, the satanic goddess of the Zisoans. Solomon not only allowed them to worship them (something strictly forbidden by God and punishable by death), he also allowed them to even make sacrifices unto them—furthering his abominable and blasphemous acts. God had appeared to Solomon and warned him not to do this twice, but yet he ignored God and still did it.

Of course all this greatly angered God. However, because of David, God had mercy upon Solomon and would not destroy him.

> *Wherefore the LORD said unto Solomon, Forasmuch as this is done of thee, and thou hast not kept my covenant and my statutes, which I have commanded thee, I will surely rend the kingdom from thee, and will give it to thy servant. Notwithstanding in thy days <u>I will not do it for David thy father's sake</u>: but I will rend it out of the hand of thy son [Rehoboam].*
>
> *Kings 11:11-13*

Because of Solomon's sins and abominations against God, God's judgment was to take the kingdom away from him. However, in the above passage, God said that because of the life of his father, David, God would not do this until the next generation. This was great for Solomon. Because although he had totally rejected and abandoned God through these satanic exploits, he still enjoyed the blessings, prosperity and peace of God in the kingdom during his life. But Solomon's son, Rehoboam was not quite so fortunate.

Rehoboam inherited Solomon's kingdom, along with his riches and fortune. He thought that he was going to enjoy a life of peace, joy, and lavishing prosperity like his father, but his life was anything but that. Almost from his inauguration, Rehoboam had trouble. No matter what he seemed to do, troubles continued to mount and escalate for him. The people abandoned him and rejected him as their king, and he lost just about all the kingdom, except for one tribe. And, with this one tribe, he was only able to reign for seventeen years. He had constant war and uprising. Through war and invading armies, he lost just about all the riches and fortune Solomon had attained.

Rehoboam was not aware however that he was under a generational curse. While Solomon experienced the blessings (generational blessings) because of the "godly" life of his father, David, Rehoboam experienced the curses (generational curses) because of the "ungodliness" of his father, Solomon (towards the end of his life). In the above passage, God pronounced a generational curse upon Rehoboam's life. Again, this was done because Solomon left from honoring, serving, and obeying God, to blatant disobedience and gross abominations. Rehoboam probably tried everything in his power to stop the landslide of troubles he experienced. But no matter how hard he tried, nothing worked.

Leaving Your Children the Blessing

I have heard people make the statement, "it's my life to live as I want to live it." That may be true to some extent. It's true to the extent that God gives us choices. We can choose God's ways and live and be blessed and prosperous in life and then also receive His eternal blessings in the afterlife.

We can also choose death (living without God) and live the way we want to live. But in choosing death, no matter what we experience in this life, the afterlife will be filled with eternal torment and misery.

Whichever we choose, we must understand that it's not only our lives we are affecting with our choices; we are also affecting the lives of our children. We work hard in life to leave our children material things such as money, houses, businesses and prestige. But the most important thing we can leave our children has nothing to do with money or prestige. The most important thing we can leave them is a generational blessing.

As we live our lives being conscious of what we are leaving our children financially, we must also live our lives being conscious of what we are leaving them spiritually. If you have been living your life selfishly, thinking only of yourself, you need to repent and make a change for the sake of your children and descendants. Ask God to forgive you of your life of sin and selfishness, and not allow your sins to be carried down to the lives of your children.

In Psalm chapter 25, David prays another prayer of repentance to God. In this prayer he asks God "not" to remember him for the sake of his unrighteousness, but rather, remember him for the sake of his righteousness. David was making this prayer not only for his life, but he was also thinking about his children. In the life of Solomon, God does just that. He remembers Solomon for the righteousness for which David had lived. As a result of David's repentance and changing his ways, his son, Solomon, was blessed with an abundance of wisdom, riches and prosperity.

On the other hand you do not find Solomon making any such prayers of repentance in his old age. His life turned selfish—enjoying his lusts and sin without care or concern about how they would affect his children. As a result, his son Rehoboam received the curses of his father instead of the blessings.

The choice of how you live your life is yours. But the results of how you live it will not only affect you, it will also affect your children, and possibly generations to come. In Deuteronomy 30:19 God gives us two choices—*choose between blessings and curses*. If we choose to live according to His Spirit and His Word, we are automatically choosing the blessings for both our lives and the lives of our children and descendants. But if we choose curses, we are not only choosing them for our lives, we are also choosing these curses for our children as well.

If you have been choosing curses in your life thus far, make a conscious effort to repent and change your ways. And instead of leaving your children the generational curses like Solomon did, you can do like David, and leave your children the generational blessings.

Chapter 8

The Root Cause of Generational Curses

We have established that generational curses are payments or punishments for a particular sin or transgression that were not paid during a person's (the culprit's) life, and were passed down to a descendant to pay instead. Generational curses could have begun in the lives of your ancestors and passed down to you, or they can begin in your life and become passed down to your descendants. But regardless of where they begin, there is always a root cause of the curse. In this chapter we will discuss many of the major root causes of both personal and generational curses. The following is a list of nine of the major causes. Following this list, we will give a breakdown and more understanding of each of them.

1. Personal, physical involvement in witchcraft, satanic practices and occultism
2. Watching demonic occult movies
3. Involvement in demonic games
4. Sexual perversions and abominations, such as homosexuality, lesbianism, pedophilia, bestiality and incest
5. Other sexual sins and strongholds

6. Profanity: self-induced curses
7. A close association with someone under a curse
8. Abuse of the body
9. Continual defiance and disobedience to God

1. Personal, Physical Involvement in Witchcraft, Satanic Practices and Occultism

> *Thou shalt not bow down thyself to* [or get involved in] *them* [witchcraft, satanic practices and occultism], *nor serve them: for I the LORD thy God am a jealous God, visiting the iniquity of the fathers upon the children unto the third and fourth generation of them that hate me.*
> Exodus 20:5

The greatest cause of generational curses is occultism and satanic practices. In this passage, God says that He sends generational curses upon them that hate Him. Satan is the enemy of God. Everything about Satan, satanic occults, and satanic practices are diametrically opposed to God, His Word and His Spirit. So to engage in any satanic practice (intentionally or unintentionally) is to make yourself an enemy against God.

It's the equivalence of trading sides and joining the side of the enemy. This is actually what happens spiritually when a person engages in this type of activity. A person's involvement in satanic activities places Satan's spirit upon them. It's the spiritual equivalent of not only changing sides in war, but also taking off your uniform and putting on the uniform of the enemy. In combat, if this happened, the person would now become an enemy and a target of those who were once their comrades and allies.

Even though the person may not say they hate God, their actions and involvement in satanic activities and practices becomes an expression of their hatred of God. And, as a result, they bring the wrath of God upon themselves and the lives of their children and descendants in the form of personal sin curses and generational curses.

2. Watching Demonic, Occult Movies

I will set no wicked thing before mine eyes... it shall not cleave to me. —*Psalm 101:3*

The secular world says that there is nothing wrong with watching violence, horror, and sex on television. Yet the more our young people watch these types of movies, the more these things become manifested in their lives, as well as the lives of adults. The world does not connect the dots because they do not understand the spiritual realm.

There used to be a time that satanic practices were hidden and concealed. But today, witchcraft and occult activities are openly practiced in movies such as the Harry Potter series. There are now movies that are so drenched in satanic occultism that they make Harry Potter look like a kindergarten story. Just go to your local video store and you will see them there. You don't have to see the movie to know what it's about. The cover openly illustrates that the movie is satanic. Some of them seem so deep in witchcraft and satanic occultism that it makes you shiver just to pass by the movie cover.

Our nation has begun a crave for demonic, occult and horror movies. These movies are not just innocent pictures on a screen; there is an atmosphere that is produced when these movies are played. It's an atmosphere that is conducive for evil and demonic spirits.

In the above passage, David identifies the problem with watching these types of movies. The problem is that these types of movies evoke evil spirits. While you willfully watch them, you are lowering your spiritual defense and opening up your spirit, allowing them to come upon, and cleave to your spirit. When a person does this, they give evil and demonic spirits an open invitation to come and cleave to them. This is why it is impossible to guard your heart and spirit against these spirits while you watch these types of movies.

We said earlier that anyone who engages in satanic and occult activity becomes an enemy against God, and opens themselves up to the wrath of God through personal and generational curses. Watching satanic, occult and horror movies does the same thing. When a person watches these kinds of movies, they are not just sitting down being entertained; they are actively engaging (in the spiritual realm) in satanic activities. This is what brings the wrath of God upon them and their children.

3. Involvement In Demonic Games

I will set no wicked thing before mine eyes...it shall not cleave to me. —Psalm 101:3

Long gone are the days of video games such as Pac Man and Donkey Kong. Today's video games are in an entirely different dimension. Today's video games are high resolution with life-like sound effects and images. Most are extremely graphically violent. Many deal with various forms of brutality, violence, assault, murder, and even illicit sex. They are also drenched in occult and satanic undercurrents. Even though they have ratings for these games, they don't work because the children simply get an older child to buy them, or they even get their parents (who are totally unaware of the content of what they are purchasing) to buy them.

Once kids get these games, they become so addicted to them, that it's almost impossible to pull them away from them. The addiction to these games comes from the nature and spirit of the game—usually violence, sex, and occultism.

It is said that the lure of some of these games carries the same addiction as a drug habit or other addictions. It's not the intrigue of the game that pulls them to keep playing them; it's the demonic activity in which they are actively engaging when they play the games.

As we said earlier, when we engage in this kind of dark practice, we put on another spirit (an evil spirit) and become enemies against God. Again, this is what brings the wrath of God and curses upon our lives and the lives of our families and children.

This is why it is so important for us to learn to be led by the spirit. As we are led by the spirit, God will lead and guide us in what to watch on television and movies, as well as the video games that are bad for our children.

I encourage parents to take an active interest in the video games their children are playing. If you are computer illiterate and do not know about them, there are groups and organizations that can help you to determine whether or not they are suitable for your children.

4. Sexual Perversions and Abominations such as Homosexuality, Lesbianism, Incest, Pedophilia and Bestiality

And first I will recompense their iniquity and their sin <u>double</u>; because they have defiled my land, they have filled mine inheritance with the carcases of their detestable and abominable things.
Jeremiah 16:18

In this passage, God says that He will require a double sin payment for those who commit detestable abominations. This double sin payment represents the eternal payment of eternity in hell, and the payment in this life of personal and generational curses. In fact, in Deuteronomy chapter 27, God actually comes out and pronounces a curse upon people who practice these types of abominations.

God hates all sin. But there are some sins that God hates even more. All throughout the Bible you find God referencing three levels of sin. One level is sin and iniquity. The second level and greater hatred of God are abominations. And, the worst of them all are the despicable sins referred to as "detestable abominations." There are others, but all the ones named above fall into that category.

Satanic groups often begin their occult meetings and practices with one or a combination of these types of detestable abominations as well as others. They do it because it becomes a conduit for the flow of evil spirits. Because these perversions suppress and kill their spirit and consciousness of God, there is nothing to stop the flow of demonic, satanic spirits from flowing through them. God destroyed Sodom and Gomorrah and wiped these two cities off the face of the earth because they openly practiced these detestable abominations as a nation without any conviction or remorse. They openly practiced homosexuality, incest, pedophilia, bestiality, and a host of other detestable abominations. God not only destroyed these wicked cities because of these sins, in Deuteronomy chapter 29, He also pronounced a curse upon their land that nothing would ever grow in these lands.

This represents what these types of abominations do to people. First, it kills their spirit and consciousness with God and His Spirit, and leaves them blinded to the truth. And, because their spirit is dead, they cannot see or hear God, and neither can they recognize the truth of His Word. They believe what they are doing is right because they have no conviction or consciousness of God to tell them they are wrong or convict them of wrongdoing. Secondly, as God pronounced a curse upon the land of Sodom and Gomorrah, a curse is also applied to those (and their descendants) who practice these abominations without any remorse or repentance.

5. Other Sexual Sins

There are other sexual sins that also bring the wrath of God upon us. They are personal sexual sins and heterosexual sins. They include illicit sex, masturbation, pornography, and voyeurism. Abortion can also be included in this category. While these and other personal and heterosexual sins may not carry the same spiritual defilement and invocation of evil spirits as the previous topic, they can still be extremely destructive to your spirit. Continued, non-repentant activity in these sexual sins can also kill your spirit and consciousness with God as well.

Although these kinds of sexual activities may be more accepted by society, they are still nonetheless sins and perversions with God. These sins bring destruction and death to your spirit. This type of death is a separation from God. Like Adam, it separates you from your intimacy, fellowship and commune with God. And, any time you become separated from God, you also become vulnerable and susceptible to the influence and oppression of evil and demonic spirits. But in addition to the spiritual death and demonic susceptibility that these sexual sins bring upon our spirit (as well as other sins we commit), there is even more spiritual danger involved.

> *What? know ye not that he which is joined to an harlot* [or any illegal sexual act] *is one body? For two, saith he, shall be one flesh. But he that is joined unto the Lord is one spirit.*
> *1 Corinthians 6:16-17*

When two people lie together in sexual promiscuity, they are taking a very big risk. Not only can a person contract sexually transmitted diseases such as HIV/AIDS through sexual contact, they can also contract other spirits. When two people have illicit sex, they join spirits with each other. Whatever spirits are on one person can become transferred to the other person. They can be any number of different kinds of spirits and ungodly addictions.

Like AIDS, these spirits lie dormant upon that person until an appropriate time before they manifest themselves. Years, and even decades later, the person begins developing bad habits and addictions they have never had before. These struggles and addictions often plague them for the rest of their lives.

In the same manner, if a person is joined together with someone who is under a generational curse, because they join spirits, that curse can also be visited upon the other person. Even though the generational curse may not have been initiated or targeted towards that particular person, their sexual connection with the person under the curse allows the spirit of the Gibeonites to also bring judgment upon them as well.

* Note: For more information about the danger and transfusing of spirits through sexual contact, please order our CD entitled, *"Fornication, Dealing with Demons."*

6. Profanity: Self-Induced Spells and Curses

In our society we openly use profanity like it's a second language. The same profanity that was once only used under the caution of a rated R movie is now heard on prime time television. Many people think that they are just using superlative expressions when they use profanity, but that's not true at all. There is a meaning behind every word of profanity. Not only is there a meaning behind every word, there is a curse given behind every phrase.

> *Death and life are in the power of the tongue...*
> *Proverbs 18:21*

When you speak profanity, you are actually speaking death to your own life and others. You are also invoking self-induced curses upon your life and family. Many of the words we use in profanity are actually shortened witchcraft curses. You don't have to be a witch or warlock to cast a spell on someone. You can be a Christian who goes to church, sings in the choir and gives tithes, and yet still use witchcraft by using profanity — and thus casting spells on people.

When we use them in regard to someone else, we are actually casting a demonic spell on them. This kind of continued activity brings the wrath of God in the form of personal and generational curses in our lives.

* Note: We have a specific message that deals with the demonic use of profanity entitled, "*The Curse of Cursing*." I implore you to please get this message. Once you get this message and understand the level of witchcraft and curses you are operating in, you will never curse again.

7. Close Associations with People Already Under a Curse

Most people think that generational curses can only be passed down to descendants of a person that were related by blood. But this is far from the truth. Generational curses can also be applied to anyone who has a close association to someone who is under a curse. The following are a few of the types of close associations that can connect a person to a generational curse:

Association of Position:

In our foundational passage, after David asked God why they continued to have the famines, God revealed to David that the source of the famine was the sin Saul committed against the Gibeonites. A lot of people have had a problem understanding this passage because they say that David was not directly related to Saul—the one who actually committed the sin.

Even though David was not responsible for the transgression against the Gibeonites, it became his responsibility to eradicate it because of the position he had taken as the new king. A generational curse can be placed upon a position instead of a family.

When Saul transgressed against the Gibeonites, he was the king. This generational curse became the responsibility of David, *not* because he was in the lineage of Saul, but because the curse was placed upon the position Saul once occupied. Even if David had not become the king, this same curse would have still come upon the Israelites, and would still have been the responsibility of the king to deal with.

Association with your Job:

When a business is established, it can be established under two charters: Sole proprietorship or Incorporation. In business, there are many legal dangers that a business can fall into. But the one I want to focus on is the problem of liability. If the business is a sole proprietorship, and someone sues the business, they sue the owner as an individual. In the case of liability, the courts can freeze or even seize the personal assets of the owner such as their cars, house, bank accounts and other assets if the conditions of the lawsuit and court settlements are not met.

But when a business is incorporated, the liability of damages is restricted to the assets owned by the company. For example: If a company gets sued for a million dollars, the courts cannot touch the personal assets of the owner of the company even if they exceed millions. In this case, the liability is limited to the company's assets and resources.

In the same manner, liability (payment) of a generational curse can be much like that of a business. The sole proprietorship represents the personal sin curse or generational curse that can touch any part of an individual's life, family or descendants. In these curses, the person, family or descendants pay for the sin personally. But the business that is incorporated represents the kind of curses that are attached to a position in the business only. In this case the curse is restricted to the person's job, business or position.

There are people who personally are not bad people, but when it comes to business, they operate like they are demonically possessed. And just as you reap what you sow personally, a company or business will also reap what it sows as a business. Sometimes the unethical, immoral, and unscrupulous dealings of a company or a position in the company are judged by God and cursed. With these curses (like the company that is incorporated), the person's personal life and family are spared from the curse, but the job, position or business will suffer the penalty. This means that whoever inherits the job, position or business is going to have continued trouble until the curse is fulfilled, or unless they learn how to break the curse.

Like David with the famine, no matter how hard they work, how business savvy they are, or how much help they attempt to attain, the business will continue to suffer or have trouble until the curse has been fulfilled. I believe that there are many people who have lost their jobs, and many businesses that have gone bankrupt and gone out of business due to no fault of their own, but due to a generational curse that was placed upon that job, position or business.

This is why if you are accepting a new job, position, or inheriting a new business, find out (if possible) the circumstances by which your predecessor left. If they were fired, or if the business sustained severe financial difficulties, and you find yourself having the same type of non-stop, redundant, problems, it could be that your job, position or business is under a curse, and you need to get deliverance.

Association By Marriage:

When you marry someone, you become joined together and connected with them as one in the spirit. This spiritual connection connects you to their blessings as well as their curses. In the Old Testament, whenever someone was judged by God, not only would they be stoned or killed, God would command that everything and everyone connected to them also be destroyed. An example of this can be found in the book of Joshua chapter seven in the story of Achan. This is the man who sinned against God by hiding the accursed garments in his tent. Because of his sin, God placed a curse upon the whole nation of Israel. Eventually God revealed to Joshua that Achan was the cause of the curse. Achan was then exposed and judged by God, and the Israelites had Achan, his wife, children, animals, and everything connected to him stoned.

We may feel that it was not fair to kill Achan's family for what he had secretly done. But had they left any remnant of Achan, the curse could have still continued upon the people. This story was also written as a picture for us as New Testament Christians. It was written to help us to understand the connection we make with people spiritually when we are joined together with them in marriage. Achan's wife and family enjoyed his prosperity, but because of Achan's sin, and their connection with him as a family, they had to also partake and share his punishment.

In chapter seven we talked about generational blessings, and how your life can be blessed by your association to a person who is under generational blessings. But in the same manner, you can also become cursed by someone close to you who is under a generational curse. If you are married to someone under a curse, because of your connection to them spiritually, their judgment may also be applied to your life. If you recognize that you are under a curse, don't just sit there and be stoned (cursed), receive God's help and deliverance and come out of it.

Association By Friendship:

In addition to receiving generational curses because of your association by marriage, you can also receive generational curses because of your close relationship and friendship with someone under a curse. You not only make a spiritual connection to people you are married to, you also make a spiritual connection to people with whom you have a close friendship or relationship.

When you establish a new relationship or make friends with someone, at some point in the friendship or relationship you open up your heart to them. Along with opening your heart to let them in, you also open up your spirit and join with them. The closer you get to them, the more the spiritual connection is solidified. When the judgment of a generational curse is handed down to them, it also connects with everyone who is closely connected with them. It's like electricity. It continues to connect and flow through every object that makes a connection with it.

8. Drug Addiction, Alcohol Addiction, and Other Destructions to the Body

Know ye not that ye are the temple of God, and that the Spirit of God dwelleth in you? If any man defile the temple of God, him shall God destroy....
1 Corinthians 3:16

Even though God gives us the liberty to choose to live as we will, our bodies are not our own to do as we will. Our bodies belong to God. In the above passage, God gives us a warning that if anyone (willfully) defiles (or does anything destructive to) the temple (our bodies), He will destroy them. This defilement refers to anything we do intentionally to our bodies that is harmful to it.

This includes the abuse of drugs (of all kinds), cigarettes, alcohol, obesity caused by overeating and overindulgence, or any other type of continual chemical, substance, or physical abuse. When I was a young Christian, I used to wonder why these types of things were considered sin when they were not spelled out as sin in the Bible. I came to understand through the Spirit that the reason they are sin is because when we do these things, we are destroying someone else's property (God's). We are commanded by God to take care of the bodies in which He has given to us to live. And, if we defile our bodies, God says that (because of our disobedience [sin]), He will bring destruction upon us. This destruction that God is referring to comes in the form of personal sin curses and generational curses. These curses are most often manifested in the form of physical sickness and disease.

Many end up paying for their sin of the destruction of God's property through personal sin curses manifested as sickness and diseases during their life. But there are some that *seem* to get away with abusing their bodies and nothing ever happens to them. Some people live well into their 80's and 90's even after abusing drugs, alcohol, cigarettes, and food for most of their lives. And, when they die, they don't even die from the kind of diseases associated with their lifelong abuse. They die of a heart attack or simply of old age.

On the other hand, you have people who diligently take care of their bodies, who do not smoke, drink, or consume drugs of any kind, watch what they eat, watch their weight, and yet they contract diseases such as cancer of the lungs and other parts of the body, kidney failure, liver damage, and other debilitating, life-threatening and even fatal diseases. Some even contract these diseases at a very young age.

This perplexity of life used to bother me before I came to understand the subject of personal and generational curses. Those who live long lives of abusing their bodies and yet do not seem to pay for their abuse do not completely get away. Many of those sins of abuse are paid for in an eternal punishment. But some are paid for by their descendants. Their descendants sometimes have to pay the price of their abuse with sickness and disease.

There are many people who have had to bear the burden of sickness and disease because one or some of their ancestors abused their bodies. The ancestor may have gotten away with a life of sin and abuse of their bodies, but the sin didn't get away. Because they died without paying the penalty for their abuse, the payment was passed down to a descendant to pay for it. Earlier we discovered that when a curse is passed down, it can branch off into other areas. Therefore, when the payments are passed down, they are not always associated with the same specific area of abuse. They can change and become manifested in any type of sickness or disease.

Please note that this is not a rule of thumb. There are many reasons why people are attacked with sickness and disease in life. Many of them have nothing to do with generational curses. But there are some that are afflicted to pay

nalty for someone else's sinful abuse. And, if this is the
you need to understand what has happened, so you
can understand what is going on, and you can also understand that God has made a way of escape and deliverance for you.

9. Continual Defiance and Disobedience to God's Word

To this point we have named eight things that cause curses to come upon our lives. But even though we have named some of the primary things, this is not all of them. A curse can come upon someone's life because of any continual, redundant sin.

> *For rebellion is as the sin of witchcraft, and stubbornness is as iniquity and idolatry. Because thou hast rejected the word of the LORD, he hath also rejected thee from being king.*
> **1 Samuel 15:23**

In this passage, God is rebuking King Saul and denouncing him as king of Israel. The reason for God's rebuke and revocation of Saul as king is because of his direct defiance and disobedience to God and His Word, and his decisions to make his own rules, instead of following God's Word and laws.

This type of rebellion occurs when a person knows what God's Word says concerning their sins, and they know they are wrong and in violation of His Word, but because of their love and lust for that particular sin, they continue in it, in spite of knowing they are in direct defiance to God and His Word. This type of stubbornness occurs when they are deep in the sin, and God attempts to speak to them about their sin, and they know God is speaking to them, but they first of all refuse to listen to the voice of God about the sin, and secondly refuse to (truly) repent of their sins.

God calls this type of rebellion "witchcraft." He also calls this type of stubbornness "idolatry." With God, there is a big difference between a person repeatedly struggling with a sin in life—who continually falls in a sin, but yet repents and asks for God's mercy, forgiveness and deliverance each time they fall, versus a person who blatantly walks in a sin without any remorse, or any sign of true conviction or repentance.

This was the biggest difference between the life of David and Saul. Both of them sinned and transgressed against God at times, but you never find anywhere in the Bible where Saul demonstrates true, heartfelt repentance. Yet each time David sinned, and God spoke to David about his sin, he humbled his heart before the Lord, cried out for forgiveness, and asked for the Lord's mercy and deliverance from the sin.

Even though both of them sinned, God accused one of them (Saul) of operating in witchcraft and idolatry, but yet commends the other (David) as being a man after His own heart, even though he too had sinned.

We can walk in this type of witchcraft and idolatry as Saul did with any sin in which we refuse to be willing to listen to God's voice about our sin, and seek repentance and His deliverance from it. When a person continually operates in this type of witchcraft and rebellion (like Saul), it can bring the wrath of God upon them, and bring personal and generational curses upon them and their descendants.

Throughout this chapter we have named and detailed many things that bring the wrath of God upon us in the form of generational curses. But now we are going to take a look at how we can get God's deliverance and escape the curse.

Chapter 9

Escaping the Spirit of the Gibeonites

Now that we have discovered what generational curses are, where they come from, and how they are passed down, it may seem quite depressing knowing that we may have to not only suffer the penalty for our sins, but also the sins of our ancestors. But in 1 Corinthians 10:13, it says that *God will always make a way of escape.* In this chapter we want to look at a man by the name of Mephibosheth. We will discover how he escaped the judgment of the Gibeonites, and therefore learn how we can also escape the spirit of the Gibeonites (generational curses).

Mephibosheth — A Picture of God's Mercy

Before I can go further into explaining the significance of Mephibosheth, I need to give you a little historical background on him. Mephibosheth was one of Saul's grandsons. He was Jonathan's son. Jonathan and David were extremely close friends. When King Saul was hunting for David to kill him because of his jealousy and envy for David, Jonathan protected David and helped him.

Jonathan knew that his father desired to kill David for no reason. He also knew that God had appointed and anointed David to be the king of Israel in the stead of his Father, Saul. He and David made a covenant that when David became king, he would bless Jonathan and his family. However, Jonathan died in battle with his father, and was never able to see David crowned as king and take advantage of the pact and covenant that he and David had made.

After David was crowned king, he wanted to keep the covenant he had made with Jonathan. He therefore sought out and found one of Saul's grandsons and Jonathan's son by the name of Mephibosheth. David brought him to live among him in his castle, blessed him, and allowed him to eat with him and his family. In essence he treated Mephibosheth with the same treatment he would have given to Jonathan.

The Law of Representation:

Here is the Law of Representation regarding this story. King David represents God who blessed Mephibosheth. Jonathan represents Jesus Christ, because it was through the death of Christ that we escape the penalty of hell, and will reign and live with God forever. Again, it was only through the death of Jonathan that Mephibosheth was able to be so blessed. Likewise we represent Mephibosheth because it was only through the death of Jesus Christ that we will live with God and be blessed by Him.

When kings ascend to the throne, they usually, immediately kill all of the former king's sons. They do this to avert any futuristic threats of one of the sons coming back to avenge their father's death and overthrow them as king.

But when David became the king in Saul's stead, he spared Mephibosheth's life because of Jonathan. Again, this is a picture of our salvation. Mephibosheth's life was spared because of Jonathan's death. We were likewise spared from death (the death of hell) because of the death of Christ.

Mercy Given Twice

> *Wherefore David said unto the Gibeonites, What shall I do for you? And wherewith shall I make the atonement, that ye may bless the inheritance of the LORD? And the Gibeonites said unto him...Let seven men of his sons be delivered unto us, and we will hang them up unto the LORD... <u>But the king spared Mephibosheth</u>...*
>
> 2 Samuel 21:3-7

Again, when David went to the Gibeonites to see how he could stop this curse, the Gibeonites asked for seven sons of Saul. At this point, David was desperate to get rid of the curse, and would have done anything to stop it. But notice verse 7, where it says, *"But the king spared Mephibosheth..."*

This is the second time Mephibosheth was spared. In the previous topic we explained how Mephibosheth should have been killed when David ascended to the throne, but because of Jonathan, David spared him. Now comes a second call for Mephibosheth's life. When David asked the Gibeonites what they would take to give a release from the curse, the only consideration they would take was for David to give them seven sons of Saul to be hung for the revenge (payment) of what Saul had done to them.

Now David could have easily grabbed Mephibosheth and given him over to the Gibeonites as one of the seven sons of Saul. Mephibosheth was conveniently right there in the castle living with him. Instead, he went out his way and searched for other sons of Saul and gave them over to the Gibeonites instead of Mephibosheth.

So Mephibosheth's life was spared twice. Now remember, we said that when we sin, there are two judgments for which we must answer. One is the eternal judgment and the other is the physical, earthly judgment. We've already discovered that Christ came to die on the cross to spare us from the spiritual, eternal judgment of hell, but this story of Mephibosheth shows us that we can also be spared from the physical, earthly judgment as well.

Remember we said that the spirit of the Gibeonites cries out to God for justice and vengeance on sin and injustice that was not paid during a person's life. If the person dies without being judged for the sin or injustice, the spirit of the Gibeonites cries out for a relative substitute to pay the penalty or punishment.

We will either be like the seven sons of Saul, or like Mephibosheth. The seven sons of Saul were judged and hung by the Gibeonites. Although these seven sons of Saul escaped the first judgment (death), they did not escape the second death. They represent those of us who (because of the spiritual Jonathan, Jesus Christ) will escape the judgment of hell and will reign with God forever. But even though these seven sons of Saul escaped the first judgment, they did not escape it the second time. They were handed over to the Gibeonites and hung by them. This represents those same people who will miss hell and go to heaven, but yet pay the penalty and judgment of the spiritual Gibeonites during their earthly, physical life.

If we come under a curse and fail to apply the principles of this book, we will be like the seven sons of Saul who escaped one judgment, but were caught and judged by the Gibeonites. This represents those who will escape the judgment of hell, but yet fall victim to generational curses in this life.

But, we can also be like Mephibosheth. Again, his life was spared twice. This represents how that through the blood of

Jesus Christ we can escape the judgment of hell. And, through knowledge and application of the biblical principles in this book, we can also escape the judgment of the Gibeonites (generational curses) for our lives, families and descendants. The choice is yours.

Chapter 10

Getting Released from the Curse

In our previous chapter we said that Mephibosheth represents God's mercy given twice. Even though we may have messed up in our lives and done some terrible things, there is still an escape from the spiritual Gibeonites we can attain though the instructions of God. Some people cannot understand or fathom the idea of being released from certain sins, especially those we consider big sins. But if we are willing to heed to God's Word and instructions, we can take advantage of the escape from the spiritual Gibeonites He has made available to us.

You've got to first of all understand that "The King" has the power to release debt, both in this life and the life to come. And, when He releases debt, healing (spiritually, physically, financially, etc.) takes place.

What Difference Does it Make

And he entered into a ship, and passed over, and came into his own city. And, behold, they brought to him a man sick of the palsy, lying on a bed: and Jesus seeing their faith said unto the sick of the palsy; Son, be of good cheer; thy sins be forgiven thee. And, behold, certain of the scribes said within themselves, this man blasphemeth. And Jesus knowing their thoughts said, wherefore think ye evil in your hearts? For whether is easier, to say, thy sins be forgiven thee; or to say, arise, and walk? But that ye may know that the Son of man hath power on earth to forgive sins, (then saith he to the sick of the palsy,) arise, take up thy bed, and go unto thine house. And he arose, and departed to his house.

Matthew 9:1-7

In this passage, the scribes were disgruntled with Jesus for healing a man. But the problem they had was not with Jesus simply healing the man (because they had seen Him heal before); the problem they had was what He said in relation to healing the man, when He said, *"thy sins be forgiven thee."* They did not believe He was the Son of God, and therefore considered it blasphemous for Him to say that the man's sins were forgiven.

Now look carefully at the correlation between Jesus saying *"thy sins be forgiven thee"* and the man receiving His healing. When Jesus tied these two things together, He was showing the relation between generational curses and sins. When Jesus told the man that his sins were forgiven, He was releasing the man of all of his sins, and the sins of his forefathers, thus releasing the man from all personal sin curses and generational curses. The release of all of his personal and generational curses also released him from all sickness and disease that were connected to, or associated with any curse, thus causing the man to be able to receive his healing.

When Jesus saw that the scribes had a problem with Him forgiving and releasing the man's sins, He then asked them this question: "Which is easier, to forgive the man's sins, or to simply heal him?" What Jesus was in essence saying was this: This man's illness was a result of a curse somewhere in his life. And as the Son of the Living God, He had the power to heal the man either through simply forgiving the man of his sins—thus releasing the man from personal and generational curses that attributed to his sickness, or simply telling the man to be healed—thus healing him by the miraculous power of God. Jesus was telling them that it did not make a difference. Either way, the end result would still be the same; the man would receive his healing.

This point is very significant if we are going to understand the power and the authority that God has to release us from generational curses. Just as Mephibosheth deserved to be judged, but was spared by David (who represents God), if we are willing to follow God's Word and directives, we can also receive a spiritual pardon, and escape the judgment of the spiritual Gibeonites.

The Price of the Atonement

> *Wherefore David said unto the Gibeonites, What shall I do for you? And wherewith shall I make the atonement, that ye may bless the inheritance of the LORD? And the Gibeonites said unto him... let seven men of his sons be delivered unto us, and we will hang them up unto the LORD in Gibeah of Saul, whom the LORD did choose. And the king said, I will give them.*
>
> *2 Samuel 21:3-4*

In this passage David asked the Gibeonites what they would take for atonement for Saul's transgressions. They asked for seven sons of Saul to be handed over to them to be hung for the revenge for Saul's atrocity against them.

In spite of Saul hunting for David like a dog to kill him, David still loved Saul. He mourned greatly at the death of Saul. David even loved Saul's sons and grandsons. He honored them and had a great deal of respect for them. It truly hurt David to his heart to have to give up these sons of Saul to the Gibeonites to be killed, but there was no other way.

These seven sons of Saul represented the atonement price that had to be paid in order to release the curse. Once a generational curse has been executed, there has to be an atonement price paid in order to release the curse before it is fully paid. We have already discovered throughout this book that there are two prices that must be paid for our sins—the physical and the spiritual. Jesus paid the eternal atonement price for our sins, but either we or our descendants have to pay the physical price for our transgressions. But we also discovered in our previous chapter that just as Mephibosheth escaped the judgment of the Gibeonites, we can also escape their judgment (generational curses).

In the story we gave of Mephibosheth, we said that David represents God, because it was ultimately up to David to both bless and release Mephibosheth. We said that Jonathan represents Jesus Christ, because it was through Jonathan's death that Mephibosheth's life was spared and blessed, and we represent Mephibosheth.

Again, Jonathan's death paved the way for Mephibosheth to escape the first judgment in the same way that Jesus' death allows us to escape the judgment of hell. But it was through the payment (the death) of the seven sons of Saul that allowed Mephibosheth to escape the death (judgment) of the Gibeonites. Again, the Gibeonites represent generational curses. The sacrifice of these seven sons of Saul became the atonement for Saul's sin, allowed Mephibosheth to escape the judgment of the Gibeonites, and caused the curse to end.

If you want to follow the blessings of Mephibosheth and also escape the judgment of the spiritual Gibeonites, you are going to have to also give "seven" sons of Saul. The seven sons of Saul represent seven things we must do in order to get our deliverance, and get set free from personal or generational curses. If there is a curse upon your life, and you are willing to do these seven things (represented by the seven sons of Saul) you too can avoid the judgment of the Gibeonites and stop generational curses in your life or family.

1. Ask God to forgive you for your sins
2. Repent of the sins of your ancestors
3. Forgive others of their offenses against you
4. Release others of their offenses against you
5. Repent to the person you offended
6. Make an atonement fast
7. Make an atonement offering

1. Repent of Your Sins

If they shall confess their iniquity... which they trespassed against me, and that also they have walked contrary unto me... Then will I remember my covenant with Jacob, and also my covenant with Isaac, and also my covenant with Abraham

will I remember; and I will remember the land.
Leviticus 26:40-42

God tells us here in the second part of this passage that He would remember His covenant with Abraham concerning us if we would do the first part—confess our sins. When a person becomes born-again, through Christ, they become the spiritual seed of Abraham. It was through Abraham that God chose to establish His covenant. In a sense, when we become born-again, we become spiritual Jews. The physical Jews think that God's blessings are only upon them. But when you become born-again, God's blessings now come upon you. This is why we have a right to claim the blessings of God's Word.

So when God says He will remember the covenant He made with Abraham, Isaac and Jacob, He is also referring to the covenant He made with us (the spiritual seed of Abraham). This covenant includes God's promise to bless us, protect us, have mercy upon us, and forgive us. But all this is contingent upon the first part, which is to confess our sins.

You can begin with the gross sins of your past. You know—the ones you haven't told anyone about. They are the abominations of your past. These are sins you name specifically. After you have searched you heart and repented of those sins, you can then begin to generalize them. For example, asking God to forgive you of your life of lust, adultery, fornication, lying, or other sins you have committed in life.

Don't forget to confess the sins you have committed since you became born-again. As Christians, we have a tendency of referring to sin as something we did in another life. But the truth is that not only did we sin before we were born-again, we have also sinned *since* we became born-again. So while you are confessing the mammoth sins you committed in your other life, don't forget to confess the ones you have also done in this life.

Finding the Specific Sin

In addition to confessing the sins of your past, you must search your heart and seek the face of God to see if the curse is because of a particular sin in your life. Now that you are dealing with getting freedom from generational curses, you must be more specific. Remember, David had to find the particular, specific offense that was committed in order to get a release. You must do the same. You must ask the Holy Spirit to search your heart and reveal to you if you are guilty of a sin or transgression that may have caused this curse.

If the Holy Spirit reveals to you that it is a sin that was committed during your lifetime, you need to begin to repent and cry out to the Lord for His mercy and forgiveness. It may even be something in which you have already repented. But if the Holy Spirit brings it back up again, it means that the repentance was not sufficient enough with God.

In biblical days, if God was either judging (or about to judge) someone for their sins, they would cry out to God in repentance for hours, and sometimes days. Some of our sins become so great with God that a simple, *"I'm sorry, and I repent"* just won't do. Sometimes God wants you to spend some time mourning and supplicating before Him for your sins.

After God judged David for his sin with Bathsheba, he wouldn't eat, and he repented and cried out to the Lord until he got a release from Him. If the Lord judges you for a sin (through a personal or generational curse), you need to do the same. You need to get alone, and be willing to mourn and cry out to Him in sorrow and repentance. You must also be willing to do this whether it takes a few minutes, an hour, a day, or even several days, until you get a release from the Holy Spirit that God is satisfied with, and has accepted your repentance. Once you have received a true release from the Holy Spirit, you can then go to the next step.

2. Repent of the Sins of your Ancestors

> *If they shall confess their iniquity, <u>and the iniquity of their fathers, with their trespass which they trespassed against me</u>, and that also they have walked contrary unto me... Then will I remember my covenant with Jacob, and also my covenant with Isaac, and also my covenant with Abraham will I remember; and I will remember the land.*
>
> Leviticus 26:40-42

This passage tells us two things we must do in order to get set free and released from generational curses upon our lives. We have already talked about the first part, which is to confess our sins. Now we want to talk about the second part, which is to also confess the sins of our ancestors.

The way that you ask God for His mercy and forgiveness is as important as the repentance itself. Most people think that the way you ask God's forgiveness for the sins of your ancestors is to separate and exclude yourself from the sins, and ask God to forgive "them" of "their" sins. After all, you weren't there; so why should you be included in something that you had nothing to do with? But even though you were not there, your genealogy includes you with their sins.

The Children of Disobedience

> *Let no man deceive you with vain words: for because of these things cometh the wrath of God upon the <u>children of disobedience</u>.*
>
> Ephesians 5:6

This passage tells us that the wrath (or punishment) of God comes upon the children of disobedience. This passage has several meanings, one of which refers to generational curses.

When your ancestors sinned against God, you became the "children" of their disobedience. You may not have been the one who actually committed the sin, or even part of the generation that initiated the sin, but because of your family line and genealogy with them, God includes you as a participator in the sin. He includes you because you become one of the descendants or children of the disobedience or sin. This is what allows the judgment of God to be handed down upon you. So again, how you repent of these sins is just as important as the repentance itself.

Because you are now the children of disobedience, the sins of the family now become your sins to repent of as much as your ancestors. Therefore, when you repent to God, you first ask Him to forgive you of the sins that you have done, but when you ask Him to forgive your ancestors, you include yourself in the sin because you are their descendant.

Those of us who understand the condition of America understand that we must pray for America. God's blessings have been upon our nation from its conception. God has been with us because in the past we have honored, reverenced, and feared the Lord. But now our nation has left the same God who has blessed us all this time, and we have turned our back on Him. We have practically become an immoral, ungodly nation. America didn't get this way overnight. It happened through generations of spiritual degradation and neglect. The only thing that has kept God from completely removing His hand of blessings and protection from our nation is the prayers of the saints.

At least once or twice a week I pray and ask for God's forgiveness and mercy upon America. When I pray for America, I pray and ask God to forgive America for "our" sins. I cry out for God's mercy and forgiveness on America as if I was the prime culprit. Because I live in America, I am of the children of disobedience (concerning our nation). I may not have personally committed the type of abominations that have almost destroyed our nation spiritually, but I am of the children of those who have, and thus the children of disobedience.

Because we are the children of disobedience, when we repent of our ancestors' sins, we must not only ask God to forgive "them" of "their" sins, we must also include ourselves. We must pray and ask God to forgive "us" of "our" sins even though we may not have done the particular sin or sins at all.

Ezra's Repentance for His Ancestors

Because of Israel's sins, God allowed them to be taken into captivity, and the temple was destroyed and the walls torn down. Years later, the Lord moved upon King Cyrus of Persia to allow the Jews to return to Jerusalem to help rebuild the temple and the walls. Ezra, the scribe, was among many of the exiles that returned to Jerusalem. Upon his return, he learned of the sins of his people and their ancestors. He then understood why God had allowed this calamity to fall upon their nation.

Once he learned of these sins, he began to tear his clothes—a sign of godly remorse, and cried out to the Lord for forgiveness for his nation and ancestors. He prayed a long prayer asking for God's mercy and forgiveness. This prayer takes place in Ezra 9:8-15. Please read it in your spare time. Ezra was a devout, God-fearing man who had not committed the sins for which he was repenting. But he was repenting and crying out to God for His mercy as if he had done them. He uses pronouns such as "we, our, and us" while referring to the sins of his ancestors even though he had not done them.

The next book of the Bible is Nehemiah. Ezra was used by God to help rebuild the temple. Nehemiah was used by God to help rebuild the walls. Nehemiah's response to the sins of his ancestors was the same as Ezra's. He was also a God-fearing man who had not committed the type of sins of which his ancestors were guilty. But yet when he cried out to the Lord for His mercy and forgiveness, he included himself in the mix. And in his prayer to the Lord, he also asked the Lord to forgive "us" of "our" sins and abominations against the Lord.

I said all that to explain how you go before the Lord to ask for His forgiveness for the sins of your ancestors. You ask for His forgiveness as a family. You do not exclude yourself because you may not have done the sins that caused the curse. Your family's genealogy connects you with the sin, thus making you the children of their disobedience. You must realize that God is judging you as a family; therefore, you must also repent as a family.

Your repentance to God on behalf of your ancestors must carry the same conviction and remorse that we talked about in the previous topic. If the sin was ancestral and not personal, you must cry out to the Lord the same way we described above in the case of a personal sin. If God is judging you for a sin of your ancestors, it means that either the sin had not been repented of at all, or the culprit(s) of the sin did not adequately repent, and God therefore had not received their repentance.

If this is the case, then you need to spend some time and begin to cry and mourn to God for your ancestors' sins. Again, as we said in the previous topic, this is something that may take you some time. It may take you hours, a day, or even days of crying out to God and repenting for your family's sins. You continue to do this until you get a release from the Holy Spirit that God has accepted your repentance.

4. Forgive Others of their Offenses Against You

We have showed through Leviticus 26:40-42 that in order to get released from generational curses, you must first confess your sins, and then confess the sins of your ancestors. The next step is to release forgiveness.

Matthew 18:23-27

The above passage reference is a parable of a king who called his servants to accountability. Upon doing this he discovered that one of them had been cheating him and taking his money. The king then ordered this man, along with his family to be put in prison. The man then begged the king's forgiveness and pleaded with him to have mercy. The king was touched with the man's apology and plea for mercy and gave the man another chance. On top of that, the king even cleared the man's debts, leaving him now owing nothing.

Matthew 18:28-34

The above passage reference is the remainder of the parable. Shortly after the king forgave his steward of the debt owed him, this same steward found a man who also owed him money. The steward then threatened to put him in jail if he didn't pay the money owed to him. The man then began to plea for mercy to the steward the same way the steward had done to the king. But instead of releasing mercy the way the king had done him, he put the man in prison to pay the debt.

The king soon heard of this incident and became enraged. He was enraged because he had forgiven the steward of his debt and spared him and his family from going to prison, but yet this same steward had not shown any mercy to someone who likewise owed him money. The king then withdrew the pardon he had given the steward and had him put in prison.

The first point that I want to bring out about this passage is that not only was the steward in danger of going to jail because of the debt he owed the king, but his entire family was also in danger of being imprisoned. The steward's spouse and children did not personally steal the king's money, but because of their relation to this steward, they were tied to him, and were therefore made responsible for suffering the punishment along with the steward. In the same manner, a generational curse can be executed against someone who did not actually commit a particular sin, but simply because of their relationship to the person.

The Spiritual Prison

The second point I want to bring out is that when someone sins or transgresses against you, they become indebted to you. You therefore become their debtor, and responsible for either releasing the debt or holding them responsible to pay the penalty for the debt or transgression. As long as you refuse to forgive them, they are held in spiritual debt. This spiritual debt is a type of spiritual prison. As long as they are in this spiritual prison, it gives the spiritual Gibeonites the right to judge them.

In the story with David, the Gibeonites refused to release and forgive the Israelites until they were judged. In the same manner, when a person refuses to forgive someone of a transgression or offense against them, it can possibly hold them in a type of spiritual prison that allows the judgment of the Gibeonites to be executed upon their life for their transgression.

If the offended person dies without ever forgiving and releasing the person, the spirit of the Gibeonites continues to rise up before God crying for judgment even long after their death.

Many generational curses have been executed because an offense was made against an individual or family, and the offended person refused to forgive and release them. The longer the person is held in unforgiveness, the longer this spirit cries out to God for vengeance and judgment until they are finally judged.

The greater the sin or offense, the louder they cry. Also, the greater the sin or offense, the longer they cry — meaning, from generation to generation. This is the reason why certain sins and transgressions such as murder, rape, sexual perversions, abominations, and abuse (physical, emotional or sexual), are almost always judged in one form or another, in one generation or another.

What Comes Around Goes Around

"What comes around goes around" is a street adage that carries the same meaning as the biblical account of *"you will reap what you sow."* In the previous topic we discovered that when someone offends or trespasses against you, you have the right to hold them in unforgiveness. And, as long as they are held in unforgiveness (a type of spiritual prison), the spirit of the Gibeonites can begin to rise up and ask God for vengeance upon them. And, the more severe the crime, sin or offense, the longer and louder it will cry for vengeance until it is paid.

This type of spiritual prison however, works both ways. When you refuse to forgive someone for an offense, not only does it allow the spirit of the Gibeonites to rise up and ask for vengeance and justice upon the descendants' lives, it also opens the door for them to begin to rise up and ask for vengeance and justice upon your life and descendants as well. As long as you hold someone in the spiritual prison of unforgiveness, the spirit of the Gibeonites can judge you for offenses you have made against others. But that's not all. It allows the spirit of the Gibeonites to also execute judgment against you for offenses that were made by your ancestors. This is why Jesus taught on forgiveness so much. It wasn't just because it's the right Christian thing to do; it's also because of what unforgiveness does to you.

Some people become so angered and enraged over an offense against them that they feel that they can never release forgiveness. But you have got to let it go—not for the person's sake, but for your own sake and the sake of your family and descendants.

Allowing the Sun to Set

Be ye angry, and sin not: let not the sun go down upon your wrath: Neither give place to the devil.
Ephesians 4:26-27

The above passage is referencing the point that we should not give any place to the devil in our lives. This passage says that we give place to the devil by allowing the sun to go down upon our wrath (anger). It's not saying that you sin by getting angry. Everybody gets angry at something. There is no one who has ever lived who didn't get angry at something. But it's what happens after you get angry that determines whether or not you sin and give place to Satan in your life. The sin comes when you let the sun go down on your wrath.

Letting the sun go down upon your wrath is to hold on to the anger day after day, week after week, and for some, even year after year, never choosing to forgive and let it go. I once heard of two sisters, who as children and teenagers were very close until the age of 19 when one of them slept with the other's boyfriend. This ignited a feud between them that lasted for fifty years. It actually lasted until they finally died. They died, never reconciling with each other, allowing this offense to destroy what should have been 50 years of sisterly love and camaraderie.

The Poison

When you allow the anger of an offense to enter into your heart, and you sleep on it night after night, day after day, it begins to cause your heart to decay. It then turns into a bitter hatred and stubborn unforgiveness.

At this point, the person's mind, heart and soul become open to hear the voice and suggestions of Satan. He begins speaking to their heart, reminding them of the offense over and over again. The more they think about it, the more angered and enraged they become, and the more their heart decays.

The next stage is that this decay in their heart now enters their spirit, and their spirit becomes poisoned. Once a person's spirit becomes poisoned, it changes their character, countenance and disposition. Unfortunately, there are many people who go to church every Sunday who have poisoned spirits. When you meet them at first they may seem loving and pleasant, but after a while, the poison in their spirit begins to ooze out.

Once a person's spirit becomes poisoned, it begins affecting other areas of their life as well. It affects their lives spiritually, socially, emotionally, and even physically. It affects them spiritually because they can never get into the holy presence of God with a poisoned spirit. They can come to church, sing hymns, and go through all types of religious motions, but they can never have true worship or intimacy with God. It affects them socially because they have trouble establishing and maintaining relationships and friendships both romantically and socially. It affects them emotionally because it hides and buries their true, inner emotions—allowing only a false shell of who they really are to be seen.

It affects them physically because once the poison gets down inside their spirit, because the spirit and body are so closely connected, it beings to corrode the body in the form of sickness and disease. I believe that this kind of unforgiveness is the root of many of our most serious diseases.

Trace It, Face It, and Erase It

At this point the person needs either a psychiatrist or a pastor who understands generational curses and poisoned spirits. A psychiatrist gets paid a lot of money to go into your past, find the poison, and help you to root it out. In order to dig this kind of poison out, you have to do three things: trace it, face it, and erase it. The psychiatrist or minister has to go back into your past to find the root. Many times they have to go all the way back to your childhood. They will get the person to talk about their parents, other relatives, and friends.

They will go from your childhood, to high school, and on to adulthood. Somewhere hidden in their life is a root of offense that has poisoned their spirit. This is the "trace it" part—locating the offense. When they locate it, there is a trigger that goes off in the person. The person's whole facial expression, countenance, and voice level and modulation sometimes change. Some psychiatrist will even put a type of lie detector apparatus on the patient that measures their pulse during this time. When the psychiatrist hits the root, the person's pulse will even rise. This lets them know they have hit the root.

The next step is to face it. They get them to face the fact that this person or situation has injured them. They do this because most of the time this offense is hidden in deep denial by the person. They have buried and covered it up by a pile of emotional camouflage where others around them cannot tell that it is even there.

The psychiatrist then gets them to "erase it" by opening up and talking about it. Sometimes this can go on for days or even weeks. Afterwards, they get the person to forgive and release the person that hurt or offended them. In our next topic we will go more into what it means to truly release someone. When forgiveness takes place, it's like giving a poisoned person an antidote. It's only then that the person can begin to recover. They can begin to recover spiritually, physically, emotionally and socially. In some cases their health will begin to drastically improve. In fact, when I pray for people who have been attacked with serious diseases, I routinely tell them to release forgiveness to those who have offended them.

When the Gibeonites forgave and released the Israelites, the curse was removed and the famine ended (land was healed). When a person forgives and releases an offender, the offended person can begin to experience healing throughout their life. If you are under a curse, go back and begin to ask God to search your heart to see if there is someone whom you have not truly forgiven. Once you are able to trace it, face it, and erase it, like David, you can be freed from generational curses and begin to experience healing in your life.

4. Release Others of Their Offenses Against You

Many people do not understand the difference between forgiveness and release. Many think that when you forgive someone that you are also automatically releasing them. Although they are very similar, there is a difference. Forgiveness is a choice of your will. Releasing someone is an action of the heart. When I say that forgiveness is a choice of your will, it's something that you choose to do out of your conscious desire and will.

You can choose to forgive someone. But because you may make a choice to forgive them does not mean that you are automatically releasing them from your heart. There are times that an offense is relatively mild, and the choice you make to forgive them can also produce a release in your heart for them.

But there are also other offenses that are so severe, and the scars and wounds from the offense are so deep, that even though you choose to forgive them, it will take time and effort to actually release them. The offended person may want to release them, but the severity of the pain from the offense causes them to indirectly hold on to the offense long after words of forgiveness may have been uttered.

The Spirit of Offense

In one of our previous topics we talked about the spirit of offense. When an offense is made, or two people get into an altercation, the spirit of offense arises. The spirit of offense is a branch of the spirit of anger. We discussed that it is not a sin to get angry. Everyone gets angry at some time in their life. But we discovered that the sin comes when we allow the sun to go down on our wrath (choose to continue to hold on to the anger).

We also stated that the spirit of offense is a type of spiritual prison. When a person is in a physical prison, they lose all their liberty and freedom. When a person is in the prison of the spirit of offense, the same thing happens.

> *Therefore if thou bring thy gift to the altar, and there rememberest that thy brother hath ought against thee; leave there thy gift before the altar, and go thy way; first be reconciled to thy brother, and then come and offer thy gift.*
> *Matthew 5:23-24*

Jesus is teaching us here about the spirit of offense. He is teaching us that when a person is in the spirit of offense, God does not hear their prayers, receive their worship, or receive their offerings and sacrifices. This is a type of spiritual prison in which you lose all your spiritual liberty and commune with God. And notice where He says, "*If thy brother hath an ought against thee...*" It doesn't matter who is at fault. It could be totally the other person's fault. There is a saying that "*two wrongs don't make a right.*" This saying is true when it comes to the spirit of offense. It doesn't matter if the other person was totally wrong or not; if you get caught up in the spirit of offense with them and refuse to both forgive and release the offense, then you become a partaker of that spirit, and become just as wrong as the offender.

The Total Release

In our previous topic we discovered that if we fail to both forgive and release someone, it holds them in spiritual prison and causes them to become vulnerable to the judgment of the spiritual Gibeonites. We also discovered that it not only holds them in spiritual prison; it also holds us in spiritual prison as well. And, while we are in spiritual prison, we also become vulnerable to the judgment of the spiritual Gibeonites, not only for our sins, but also for our ancestors' sins. This is why it is so important for you to learn to not only forgive people who have offended you, but to also seek the Lord until you get a total release. The release is not only for them, it's just as much for you.

If you are under a generational curse, you must ask the Holy Spirit to help you to search your heart to see if there is anyone in your life who has wounded you with an offense that you have not been able to totally release. You may have said you forgave them, or may have even told the person you forgave them, but yet in your heart you have not truly released them yet.

Many times we need the Holy Spirit to reveal this type of offense to us. And, once the Holy Spirit reveals it to us, it also takes the supernatural help of the Holy Spirit to help us to actually release them. When someone has deeply wounded us, we often cover the offense by attempting to forget it as quickly as we can. Time can help us to cover the offense where the sting and pain no longer bother us as bad, but underneath the cover, the offense is still as strong. All it takes is a moderate reminder of the incident, and the pain resurfaces. Although you may want to release them, the severity of the wound causes your heart to continue to hold on to the offense. Without the supernatural intervention and help of the Holy Spirit, you may hold on to this offense for the rest of your life, even though you may have said you forgave the person.

One of the ways you can tell that you have not truly released a person yet is when it terribly bothers or grieves you to be around the offender, think about them, or even hear their name mentioned. If their name or presence still bothers or grieves you, you have only covered up the offense, and you need to get a release.

Another way you can tell if an offense still bothers you is if you desire for them to get rewarded for what they did to you. I often hear Christians say, *"they are going to get theirs."* They say this in regard to an offender, hoping that God will reward them evil (pay them back) for the wrong or transgression done to them. If you have thought, said, or even hoped this for someone who has offended you, then you have not truly released them.

> *And they stoned Stephen, calling upon God, and saying, Lord Jesus, receive my spirit. And he kneeled down, and cried with a loud voice, Lord,*

lay not this sin to their charge. And when he had said this, he fell asleep [died].

Acts 7:59-60

In this passage they stoned Stephen for preaching the Gospel of Jesus Christ. While dying, he asked the Lord to not lay this sin to their charge. He was in essence asking God to not only forgive and release them from this sin, but to also not even cause anything to happen to them in their physical life as a payback for their transgression against him.

Again, when you say, desire, or hope someone gets paid back for an offense against you, you have not truly released them. You are still holding them in spiritual prison, giving the spiritual Gibeonites the right to come and bring judgment upon them. But again, it also gives them the same right to bring judgment upon your life and family for offenses both you and your ancestors have made against others. But when you choose to both forgive and totally release others for their sins and transgressions against you, it also releases you from the judgment of the Gibeonites for sin and transgressions both you and your ancestors have committed.

When Jesus was on the cross, He asked God to forgive those who had crucified Him. He did this for two reasons. First, He knew that they did not believe or realize they had actually brutally tortured and murdered the Son of the Living God. He knew that the payment for this sin would have cursed their descendants for centuries to come. Now even though they still had to pay the eternal penalty for their sins, Christ's forgiveness released and spared their descendants from some devastating curses.

The second reason He did it was because He could not go to the grave in the spirit of offense. In our previous topic we quoted Ephesians 4:26-27 that tells us *not to give place to the devil by allowing the sun to go down upon our wrath.* People who die holding on to offenses place themselves in a very dangerous position when they stand before God. It's dangerous because of this: God forgives and covers our sins based upon us forgiving and releasing others of their sins. An example of this biblical concept can be found in the parable we used in the previous topic about the king and his steward.

People who go to their grave intentionally refusing to forgive and release others risk standing before God and having Him to hold them accountable (not forgiving them) for some of their sins. And, if we have to stand accountable to God for any of our sins, then hell is our eternal destiny. Even though Christ did not have any sins, he forgave and released them to show us that we need to do the same.

Prayer — The Key to the Release

In 1979 one of my brothers was brutally shot and killed by someone. Although the person was guilty beyond a shadow of doubt, they only did a few years in prison. After I became born-again, I learned that I must forgive everyone, so I forgave them. But even though I said that I forgave this person, I didn't discover until years later that I still held on to the offense of them killing my brother. Even though I wanted to release them, it was very difficult to do so.

I later began seeking the Lord as to how I could totally release them. It was then that God gave me the well-known passage in Matthew 5:44 which tells us to *"pray for them which despitefully use us and persecute us."* At that time this was something that I definitely did not feel like doing. But I did not do it because I wanted to, but because I knew I needed to.

Prayer produces intimacy. When you pray, you become intimate with the One you are praying to (God), the one you are praying with, and the one you are praying for. When you spend time praying for someone, the intimacy of your prayers begins to pull down the walls of offense.

After the Lord showed me this, I began praying for them on a routine basis. I will not lie; it took some time. But as I continued to pray for them, eventually, the grievous walls of offense came down, and I was able to truly release them from the offense. In fact, I was later able to talk with them on several occasions and not feel any anger, resentment or ill-will in my heart towards them. This was done through the Word of God. The Word of God transforms both our heart and our minds.

Again, prayer is the key to getting a total release. If the Holy Spirit reveals someone in your past to you that you have not both forgiven and released, begin praying for them until you get a total release. You may choose to pray for their salvation, and that God would save them and help them to grow and mature in Him. And pray for whatever else God leads you to pray for.

The key in this prayer is not so much what you are saying, as much as what you are doing. It's the process of you praying for them that generates the spiritual intimacy that causes the release. Put them on your prayer list to pray for them once a week at least. The Holy Spirit will let you know by His peace when the spirit of offense has been broken and you have released them.

And, over a period of time, you will be able to not only forgive them, but also truly release them from your heart. And, once you are able to release them, then you are on your way to getting released from the curses that may have plagued your life or family.

* Note: God commands us to forgive and release those who have offended us, but He never commanded us to trust them again, or put ourselves in a vulnerable position to become victimized by them again. You don't have to trust them, allow them into the intimacy of your heart, or even allow them into the intimacy of your home, but for your sake and the sake of your family, you must forgive and release them.

5. Repent to the Person You Offended

Wherefore David said unto the Gibeonites, What shall I do for you? and wherewith shall I make the atonement, that ye may bless the inheritance of the LORD?

2 Samuel 21:3

Let seven men of his sons be delivered unto us, and we will hang them up unto the LORD in Gibeah of Saul, whom the LORD did choose. And the king said, I will give them.

2 Samuel 21:6

Humble Yourself

After David sought the face of the Lord, God gave him the answer that the generational curse was placed upon them because of an offense to the Gibeonites. In the above passage, you find David going to the Gibeonites and asking them what he could do to make it right with them.

They asked for seven sons of Saul to be handed over to them. Although David did not want to do it, he gave them what they requested. Seven sons and grandsons of Saul were handed over to the Gibeonites, who hung them. After they were hung, the judgment was fulfilled and the famine was lifted from the land.

The point I want to bring out in the above passage is that although David was the mighty king of Israel, and the Gibeonites were only servants to the Israelites, he had to humble himself and go to the Gibeonites to get the curse lifted. And, even though the Bible doesn't spell it out, it's clearly assumed that since God told David that the source of the curse was because of an offense made by Saul against the

Gibeonites, that David humbled his heart and went and repented and apologized to them.

He didn't refuse to do it because he was the king. He knew that his position had nothing to do with what he needed to do. He knew that humbling his heart and apologizing to the Gibeonites (even though the Gibeonites were their servants) was the only way to get released from the curse. Just as David didn't let his pride keep him from humbling his heart and making it right, don't let your pride keep you from humbling yourself and making it right with someone whom you may have offended.

If after you search your heart and the Holy Spirit reveals to you that the you are under a curse because of an offense you committed, you must humble your heart and go to them and apologize.

Go to the Source

Confess your faults one to another, and pray one for another, <u>that ye may be healed</u>...

James 5:16

Some religions use this passage to say that you must go and confess your sins to the pastor or priest. Sometimes it may be necessary to discuss certain issues with a pastor or priest in order to get spiritual guidance, but you never have to confess sins to a pastor or priest unless they were the one you offended. It is necessary to confess your sins to God. But after God, the only person whom you need to confess your fault or sin to is the person whom you offended.

Most people who either do not understand or do not believe in generational curses will tell you that all you have to do is to repent to God for your sins. But there's more to it than that. If you have been hit with a generational curse upon your life or family, and you want to get deliverance, you are going to have to do the same thing that David had to do—go to the source of the offense and make it right. I'm sure David and his people prayed throughout the first and second year of the famine. But again, it wasn't until they went to the source and got it right with the Gibeonites that the famine was lifted.

Now look at the third part of this passage where it says, **"*that ye may be healed.*"** When you go to the source and make it right with them (and they release you), healing takes place. David's land was healed because he went to the source and made it right. Likewise, your life, health, family or situation can also be healed by you going to the source and making it right.

Begin by truly searching your heart as to the people you have offended in your lifetime. If you truly search your heart, your conscious will reveal them to you. But, if you still do not know, pray and ask the Lord. John 14:26 tells us that *the Holy Spirit will bring all things to our remembrance.* If you really want to know, the Holy Spirit will cause you to remember the person whom you offended.

Serious offenses are never forgotten. Most of us can remember every serious offense we have had against us all the way back to our childhood. Once you find the person whom you offended, begin by letting them know that you are now a Christian. Let them know that you have made a lot of mistakes in your life. Let them know that you offended them of whatever the offense was, and that you have already repented to the Lord, but you want to also make things right with them. Ask them if they would forgive you of what you've done.

Make sure the apology is very heart-felt and authentic. Remember their forgiveness and release is the key to you getting your release. If the person does not feel that the apology was authentic, they will either not forgive you, or will say that they forgive you and not release you, still holding the grudge, thus keeping the curse active.

When someone apologizes to another person, most people with any type of adult maturity will forgive them. If the offense was really heart wrenching, you may have to sit there and listen to them tell you how much it hurt them. If they do this, do not attempt to justify yourself or give reason for the offense, just continue to be apologetic until you are finished. David didn't make any excuses for Saul, he just accepted the responsibility and did as they requested. You must do the same.

What If They Will Not Forgive You?

<u>If it be possible, as much as lieth in you</u>, live peaceably with all men.
Romans 12:18
Finally, brethren, pray for us... that we may be delivered from <u>unreasonable</u> and wicked men: for all men have not faith.
2 Thessalonians 3:1-2

There are situations where the offended person may (because of the severity of the offense to them) choose to strongly hold on to the hurt or offense and not want to see the person who offended them, speak to them, or have anything whatsoever to do with them. And, some would rather die and take it to the grave with them than to ever even think about forgiving the person who offended them.

These two passages cover these types of situations. The first passage tells us to do it (go to them) *"if it's possible."* The second passage tells us that there will be some people who will be totally *"unreasonable."* These two passages apply to the people to whom it is "impossible" to go to make it right because they are unreasonable and do not want to accept your apology.

In these types of situations it will not be possible to do this step. But because they refuse to forgive or release you does not mean that you are forced to endure the penalties with no way out. Your sincere attempt to go to them to resolve the matter is all that God requires of you. But that's not quite all there is to it. If the person refuses to reconcile or make peace with you, you must then do the previous steps we have already named, and then you must also give a double atonement offering. See the next chapter for the explanation of the atonement offerings. Once this is done, you are released from the responsibility of getting a release from them.

What If the Person Cannot be Found or is Deceased?

If you have truly, diligently searched for the person and cannot find them, or if the person is deceased, you can still get a release by making a double atonement offering. Please see our next chapter to understand more about the atonement offering.

In our foundational passage, David went to the Gibeonites' grandchildren to get a release. Some people use this as a mandate reference to say that after a person is deceased, you must go to their children or grandchildren to get a release. This is not necessarily true.

Some offenses are so severe that they are repeated and carried from generation to generation. If the offense is a known one that has been carried to the next generation (as was the case with David), it may be necessary in some extreme cases to actually go to one or some of the descendants and ask for forgiveness on behalf of your ancestor that caused the offense. But in most cases this is not the route to take.

Most of the time the children and grandchildren are not even aware of the incident. They therefore do not hold the grudge or unforgiveness. If you reveal to them the offense that took place in another generation, it is going to only stir up bitterness, resentment and strife for you — something they may not have had for you prior to your disclosure. So in these cases, I believe the Lord would have you to do the double atonement offering instead.

Covering a Transgression with Love

Let me give this caution: This point of having to go to the source to make it right only applies to the time when God gives you a clear word that you are under a personal or generational curse for a "specific" sin or transgression, and directs you to go to the "specific" source to make it right. Sometimes people go through personal or generational curses in life, and in order to get their hearts right with God, they attempt to go back in their lives and confess everything they have done to everyone they have wronged or transgressed. While this is a very noble thing to do, it is not necessarily scriptural. There are some situations and circumstances where telling the truth can be more hurting, damaging and destructive than to just continue to keep it covered.

> *He that covereth a transgression seeketh love; but he that repeateth a matter separateth very friends.*
> *Proverbs 17:9*

There are some things that are better left covered (not revealed or confessed to the person offended or transgressed), rather than to reveal the truth to them. I know this sounds like somewhat of a contradiction to the things we have stated earlier with this point, but it is sometimes necessary.

Let me give you an example of what I am referring to: Let's suppose a woman had lied to a man and maliciously misled him to believe he was the father of her child. Let's say that the father had bonded with the child for seven years.

Let's say that after the seven years, the mother discovered that she was under a generational curse and wanted to get things right in her life. In this case, I would suggest some serious prayer and fasting in order to get clear directives from the Lord. There are some "extreme" cases where the Lord may give the directive to reveal the truth. However, unless the Lord directly, clearly reveals that this specific transgression must be exposed, and that the truth "must" be revealed to the person transgressed, this may be a case the above passage is referring to, and it may need to be kept covered and concealed.

There is even a law in our nation regarding this kind of act. If a man has acknowledged paternity, and has begun supporting the child, but later finds that he is not the biological father at all, he has to still pay child support until the child is eighteen years of age. Of course this is not a very popular or favorable law with the men who have been deceived in this kind of act, but it was established for a purpose.

The purpose is to cover the child. Regardless of the mother's unscrupulous motive to falsely accuse the father, the revelation of this deception will also hurt the child. By this time the child has had time to bond with the man as her father, and suddenly ripping him out of the child's life will hurt the child. This law was placed in effect not as much for financial support, as it was to hopefully encourage continued emotional and parental support by the (alleged) father. This kind of support has probably been well established by this time, and to suddenly rip it from the child could cause drastic emotional problems for the child.

As the above passage is showing, it is sometimes better to cover a transgression (keep it concealed), than it is to reveal it. The motive of this concealment "must" however be love. This passage is not for those who simply do not want to be embarrassed, exposed or caught in their sin or transgression. It's for those who realize their transgression, but because of the motive of love for those who would be hurt or devastated by the revelation of the transgression, they choose to cover or conceal it.

In these types of cases, if the person feels the need to relieve their conscious by confessing the sin, this is where their pastor, priest or minister comes in. The pastor, priest or minister cannot forgive them of the sin or transgression, but they can serve as a listening ear for them to confess it to help relieve them of their burden.

If after much prayer and fasting over this matter, the Lord directs you to cover and conceal a transgression, <u>you are still required to pay a double atonement offering</u>. Double atonement offerings are required in the case where either the person is not available, or they refuse to release forgiveness. This scenario would therefore be applicable for this case.

Be careful not to use this point as avoidance from having to face or confront the person you have offended. Again, this point only applies to offenses where others are involved, and no one knows that the offense has even take place. In the case where you are under a personal or generational curse, and God has revealed to you that a particular incident is the cause of it, if at all possible, you need to go to the source and make it right.

What if the Offense Cannot be Found or Traced?

There are times that people realize that they are under a curse, and both search their hearts and diligently seek the Lord for the cause or source of the curse, but cannot seem to pinpoint the particular offense or person to whom the particular offense was made.

Sometimes it is difficult to locate the person or offense because the offense was too far in the past and the offender is unable to remember it. Sometimes it's because it was such a minor infraction to the offender (although it was an enormous offense to the person) they cannot remember it. Sometimes it is difficult to recall the offense simply because the offender didn't even realize they had hurt or offended the person. And sometimes the offense was made by one of your ancestors, and unless God reveals the specific offense to you, you have no way of knowing the specifics or nature of the true offense that caused the curse.

If either of these are your case, and you have honestly searched your heart and sought the Lord for the specific offense and cannot locate it, I strongly suggest that you do not go through life apologizing to everyone whom you have ever met.

You may be familiar with the saying, *"let sleeping dogs lie."* In other words, if you were trying to tiptoe through a pack of wild, ferocious dogs, try your best not to disturb them; because if you disturb the sleeping dogs, they may all wake up and attack you. The meaning of this saying simply means that there are some situations better left alone. As we mentioned in the previous topic, sometimes apologizing and repenting to the wrong person will only stir up strife and hatred (thus putting you deeper in spiritual prison) that was never there in the first place.

This is why it is so important for you to do like David, and diligently seek the Lord as to the person and specific offense. I'm sure David made hundreds, if not thousands of enemies in his tenure as king, and in their quest to take the land from their enemies. But you only find him going to the one (the Gibeonites) to whom God instructed.

I'm not saying that you should not apologize to people you have truly offended. Because if the Holy Ghost identifies a specific offense to you, you will not get deliverance from the curse unless you go to the person and make it right with them. I'm simply cautioning you not to go on a life exploration of apologizing to everyone you have met, thus making some matters worse, and placing yourself deeper into spiritual prison.

If this is your case, and you have truly searched your heart and sought the face of the Lord for the source of the offense and cannot find it, then instead of you making your atonement through an apology, you would go to the next chapter, and make a double atonement offering.

─────── Chapter 11 ───────

The Atonement

In our previous chapter we said that the seven sons of Saul represent seven sacrifices we must make if we want to get rid of generational curses. Up to this point most people wouldn't have a problem with the five things we have discussed thus far. The reason why most people would not have a problem with them is because they do not require any significant, personal sacrifice. But for many, the last two steps may be the most difficult because of the personal sacrifices that are required.

The Atonement

I know that many people teach that all you have to do is pray and ask for forgiveness. Repenting and asking for forgiveness is only part of what you must do to get things right when there is a curse. But if the curse is to be lifted, just as David had to pay an atonement of seven sons of Saul to the

Gibeonites, we too must be willing to pay a price. And, the price we pay for these last two points has got to cost us something.

> ...*And Araunah said unto David, Let my lord the king take and offer up what seemeth good unto him: behold, here be oxen for burnt sacrifice, and threshing instruments and other instruments of the oxen for wood. All these things did Araunah, as a king, give unto the king. And Araunah said unto the king, The LORD thy God accept thee. And the king said unto Araunah, nay; but I will surely buy it of thee at a price: <u>neither will I offer burnt offerings unto the LORD my God of that which doth cost me nothing</u>. So David bought the threshingfloor and the oxen for fifty shekels of silver.*
>
> 2 Samuel 24:21-24

In 2 Samuel chapter 24, God judged David for the sins of conceit and pride in his heart. Because of David's sins, seventy thousand men died of a plague. David wanted to make atonement to God for his sins. The place he chose to make his atonement was owned by a man by the name of Araunah.

When Araunah found that King David was on his land to make atonement for the plague that had swept the nation, he offered to give David the animals and materials he needed to build the altar and make the sacrifice free of charge. But David understood that in order for his atonement offering to be accepted by God, it had to cost him something. So he refused to accept it for free, and gladly paid the full price for what he needed to make the sacrifice.

After David made an (acceptable) atonement offering, the plague was then lifted. Likewise, if we are going to make an acceptable offering to atone for either our sins or the sins of our ancestors, it is going to cost us something.

> *And the priest shall <u>make an atonement</u> for him before the LORD: and <u>it shall be forgiven him</u> for any thing of all that he hath done in trespassing therein.*
> *Leviticus 6:7*

Just as the atonement that David gave to the Gibeonites released them from their curse, our atonement to our High Priest (Jesus Christ) shall also release us from our (and our ancestors') curses.

As I searched the Bible on atonement offerings, I found the books of Exodus and Leviticus were filled with atonement offerings. As I sought the face of the Lord concerning what would be an acceptable atonement offering for a personal or generational curse, the Lord gave me the following two steps. These two things represent the final two steps (numbers six and seven) of the price we must pay to atone for the curse.

6. A Seven Day Atonement Fast
7. A Seven Day Atonement Offering

Why the Number Seven?

> *Let "<u>seven</u>" men of his sons be delivered unto us...*
> *2 Samuel 21:6*

The Gibeonites asked for "seven" sons of Saul. The number "seven" represents completion. The seven tasks we must do represent the seven sons of Saul that had to be sacrificed. The number seven in relation to these final two tasks represents the complete payment and atonement. If you are under a curse, then you want it to be completely over. So I believe that the Spirit of the Lord is saying that you need seven of each of these to get complete deliverance.

6. A Seven Day Fast

And when he was come into the house, his disciples asked him privately, Why could not we cast him out? And he said unto them, this kind can come forth by nothing, but by prayer and fasting.
                                                    Mark 9:28-29

In this passage a man had brought his son to Jesus' disciples to cast a devil out of him. His disciples however could not cast it out. So the man took his child to Jesus, who immediately cast the devil out of his child. Afterwards, Jesus' disciples asked Him why they could not cast the devil out of the child. Jesus answered by telling them that some of our deliverances will only come by fasting and prayer.

I know we don't hear much about prayer and fasting anymore, but it is still just as relevant and needful today as it was in biblical days. In the above passage, Jesus was teaching that there are some strongholds that will not be broken with prayer alone. Some will only be broken with the combination of fasting and prayer. Personal and generational curses are types of strongholds. I believe that they fit into the category of *"this kind"* when Jesus referred to the need for prayer and fasting.

I believe that this is one of the main reasons why many generational curses are not broken in our lives. It's because we are simply too spiritually lazy and don't want to pay the price. It's easier to be like the ostrich and just stick our heads in the sand and refuse to believe that generational curses exist. And, if we do believe they exist, we want to get rid of the curse the easy way by finding a prayer line somewhere and have someone to pray over us and release us from the curse. But again, just as David had to pay a price to the Gibeonites to get deliverance from his curse, if we are going to get our deliverance, we must also be willing to pay the price.

> *...the children of Israel were assembled with fasting... and stood and confessed their sins...*
> *Nehemiah 9:1-2*

In this passage, the Israelites had been taken captive and were under oppression. Because of the sins of their ancestors, this generation now had to pay for their ancestors' sins. They realized their sins as a nation. But they not only repented, they also fasted. Throughout the Bible in the Old and New Testaments, you find prophets and other leaders tearing their clothes and putting on sackcloth and ashes. They often did this as a sign of their remorse for their sins and their broken heart to God because of sin and unrighteousness. Fasting is an outward expression to God of our remorse, broken heartedness, and repentance for sin.

In the above passage they were doing just that. Their fasting became a type of atonement, expressing their heart of remorse and penance for their sins. In this passage, God heard their cry, forgave their sins, and delivered them. In the same manner, when we fast, we are also expressing our heart-felt remorse to God for our (and our ancestors') sins. And, just as God forgave and delivered them because of their expressions of remorse for their sins, He will also do the same for us.

> *But when he saw many of the Pharisees and Sadducees come to his baptism, he said unto them, O generation of vipers, who hath warned you to flee from the wrath to come? Bring forth therefore <u>fruits meet for repentance</u>.*
> *Matthew 3:7-8*

In this passage, John the Baptist was admonishing the Pharisees and Sadducees to change and repent of their evil ways. He also told them that in addition to their need to repent, they also needed to offer up "fruits" of their repentance.

The baptism of John the Baptist was somewhat different than the baptism taught by the disciples and the baptism we do today. John's baptism was a baptism of repentance. His baptism was a type of fruit of their repentance. Fruits or works of repentance are something you do outwardly as an expression to God of your godly sorrow for your sins.

If you are under a generational curse, and you want to be released from the curse, repentance is the first step, but fasting becomes a fruit of your repentance from the heart. In the previous passage in Nehemiah, when they not only confessed their sins, but fasted along with their repentance, God heard their cry of repentance and began to restore their land. Your seven day fast will likewise be the next step toward you getting set free from the generational curse and receiving restoration in your land (your life and family's lives).

* Please Note: There are different types of fasts. I do not recommend the absolute fast for seven days. I recommend the liquid and juice fast or partial fast. For more information on fasting and the different types of fasts, please see our book entitled, *"The Warfare of Fasting."*

7. A Week's (Seven Days) Pay

As you research the scriptures in Exodus and Leviticus regarding atonement, you will always find them giving something. When it came to making atonement for their sins, they had to give animal sacrifices. The animal sacrifices represented two things: It represented the shedding of blood, which was a picture of the blood of Jesus Christ that was to be shed for their eternal sins, and it represented the payment or atonement for their sins. Here again is the two-fold payment. The animal's blood covered the sin, but there was still a personal price or cost to the person.

> *And it shall be, when he shall be guilty in one of these things, that he shall <u>confess that he hath sinned</u> in that thing: "<u>And</u>" he shall <u>bring his trespass offering</u> unto the LORD for his sin which he hath sinned, a female from the flock, a lamb or a kid of the goats, for a sin offering; and the priest shall make an atonement for him concerning his sin.*
>
> *Leviticus 5:5-6*

Notice in this passage, God first commanded that they confess their sins (which is to repent). But "in addition" to their repentance, God also commanded that they make a sin offering for the atonement of their sins.

In the same manner, if we are under a curse, we too must repent and confess our sins and the sins of our ancestors. And thanks be to God, the blood of Jesus Christ covers our sins. But if we want to get released from the curse, we must do more than repent; we must also pay atonement for the sin or sins that caused the curse in the beginning. This atonement becomes the personal price that you pay to atone for the physical sin itself. Again, the blood of Jesus Christ covers you from having to pay the eternal sin penalty; but if you want to get rid of the curse, just as it cost David something—even though he had greatly repented, it is likewise going to cost you something.

The animals they sacrificed were quite costly during those days. A lamb, goat or bullock was the equivalent to a week of work or a week's pay for an entire family. It was expensive, but it was the price they had to pay to atone for their sins.

So again, they made their atonement by giving and sacrificing a lamb, goat or bull—the equivalence of a week's pay. In addition to our repentance, we must also atone the same way if we want to get released from the curse. But instead of giving the animal, we are to give a literal week's pay to atone for the sin that caused the personal or generational curse.

I know that many will argue this point and say that our repentance should be enough, and that we should not have to give a week's pay. Our godly sorrow and repentance is enough to cover our eternal sins. Once the blood of Jesus Christ has been applied to the sin (through our repentance), it is totally paid in full. But as we have taught throughout this book, the physical, earthly penalty still has to be paid, or the curse will continue until it has been fulfilled. The week's pay becomes the final atonement (number seven) representing the seven sons of Saul that David had to give to be sacrificed to get set free from the curse that was upon he and the Israelites.

As you prepare to give this offering, do not give it grudgingly; give it in faith and with joy, knowing that through your obedience to the Word of God, the curse has been lifted, and you (and your family) have been released and set free from the curse.

As you prepare to give your atonement offering, seek the face of the Lord as to where to give it. Some are led to give it to their local church; some are led to give it to another ministry that God has placed upon their heart; some are led to give it to someone whom they know that is in need; some even feel led to give it anonymously to either the person or a family member of the offended person. Whomever you choose to give it to, be prayerful and the Lord will lead you.

Sometimes in church when we are asked to give to special projects, we simply shuffle money. In other words, if we were asked to give fifty dollars towards a special project, we simply substitute fifty dollars that we were previously planning to give in tithes or offering, and give it to the special project instead. This way, we are not out of any more money than we had planned to give in the first place.

But be very careful not to make this mistake when you are making your atonement offering. Your atonement offering is "in addition" to your tithes and regular offering. If you simply shuffle money and substitute your tithes and your normal giving, God will not accept your atonement offering, and the curse will therefore continue and not be lifted.

A Lesser Way Out

Some would look at this chapter dealing with atonement offerings and say that these last two points are too hard. Some can barely fast beyond one meal, and would see it impossible to sustain any kind of fast for seven days. Others barely make it from paycheck to paycheck, and would look at giving a week's pay to be totally devastating. If you feel that either of these two requirements are too difficult for you and your situation, then seek the face of God for a lesser way out.

> *And if he be not able to bring a lamb, then he shall bring for his trespass, which he hath committed, two turtledoves, or two young pigeons, unto the LORD; one for a sin offering, and the other for a burnt offering.*
>
> *Leviticus 5:7*

For people who were not able to afford to give a lamb, goat or bullock to atone for their sins in those days, God gave an allowance for them to bring two doves or young pigeons instead. Obviously, two pigeons were far less costly and expensive than the other animals named above, but God made this allowance for those who were poor and "truly" (couldn't afford) didn't have a lamb, goat or bullock they could sacrifice.

If this is your situation, and you truly cannot afford to give a week's pay, pray and ask the Lord if He would accept a lesser offering for you to give as an atonement offering.

Instead of giving one week's pay, He may release you to only give a couple of days' pay, or some significantly smaller amount than the week's pay.

With regard to the fast, there are different types of fasts. In our book, "*The Warfare of Fasting,*" we list six different types of fasts. Some of these fasts are very difficult to sustain, while others are much easier, and allow you to eat or drink certain things while on the fast. As you pray and ask God, He will give you a peace about which type of fast He will accept in order to break the curse against your life or family. If God gives you a peace about giving a lesser amount in either the atonement fast or atonement offering, be committed.

I would like to give a caution on this subject. I emphasized above that this "lesser way out" was only established by God for those who were poor and (truly) unable to pay the full price. This allowance was not meant to simply make it easier or less expensive to pay the atonement. David understood this principle, which is why he insisted on paying the full amount. Before you automatically jump on the lesser way out, make sure that you diligently seek the face of the Lord and get a clear directive from Him allowing you to take this route. If you have any doubt in your heart or mind, go ahead and do like David and pay the full price.

The Double Atonement Offering

In chapter ten we noted four things that would require you to give a double atonement offering. They are as follows:

1. The person you offended refuses to either forgive or release you.

2. Either you cannot locate the person whom you offended, or they are deceased.

3. You have truly searched your heart and sought the Lord, but cannot clearly pinpoint the offense that caused the generational curse.

4. You have determined that this is a transgression that is better left covered for the sake of others involved. And, your concern is motivated by love and compassion.

Basically, the double atonement offering is needful when you cannot complete step five of getting deliverance from generational curses. This step is to do like David did and go to the source and apologize to them and make it right. If any of the four circumstances apply to you, then you can replace that step by making a double atonement offering of both the atonement fast and atonement offering.

The double atonement offering is exactly what it says: you make double the atonement for the offense. Instead of giving one week's pay and fasting seven days, you give two weeks' pay and fast for 14 days.

Be careful not to lessen the atonement you are making because you have to give double. Again, the topic entitled, "A Lesser Way Out" (Leviticus 5:7) was not established by God to simply make it easier for those who don't want to pay the full price, but rather, to make it available for those who didn't have the means to give the required price. Therefore, you do not have to do it all at one time. These segments may be separated by weeks or even months if you choose to do so in order to recover from the first set of atonement offerings.

Once you have completed all seven of these steps, you have fulfilled the requirements of the Lord for His release. All that's left at this point is to go to the next chapter and make your closing prayer.

Chapter 12

Implementing the Seven Sons of Saul

Throughout this book we have discovered that personal and generational curses still exist. We have also discovered how David received deliverance from his curse when he offered the seven sons of Saul—representing to us the seven things we must do in order to get our deliverance from curses against our lives and family. A review of the seven steps we have discussed is as follows:

1. Ask God to Forgive You for Your Sins
2. Repent For the Sins of Your Ancestors
3. Forgive Others
4. Release Others
5. Apologize to Others Whom You Have Offended
6. Make an Atonement Fast
7. Make an Atonement Offering

In chapters ten and eleven we gave instructions on these seven things that must be done. But in this chapter I want to reemphasize some of the points and also give some guidance on how to implement these seven steps in order to properly get your release.

Beginning Prayer

Before you begin to implement these seven things, pray a prayer of consecration to the Lord for them. The following is a prayer you may pray, or you may pray one of your own:

Father, I come boldly before Your throne of grace thanking You for the understanding You have given me concerning generational curses, and how to get released from them. You said in Your Word that as I come to know the truth — which is to intimately learn, receive and implement the truths, precepts and revelation of Your Word in my life, that You would set me free, through the power, anointing, and deliverance of Your Word.

I now commit the task of implementing these seven things (representing the seven sons of Saul) unto you. I pray that You would give me Your anointing, strength, boldness and wisdom to implement and complete each of these tasks. And, when I finish them all, I pray that as You released David and the Israelites from the curse that was against them, that You would also release me from the curse that is against me. I commit them to You now, in the name of Jesus Christ I pray. Amen.

Implementing the Seven Points

Before implementing each point, say a short prayer, consecrating that point to the Lord. In Your prayer, ask again for God's anointing, strength, and the guidance of the Holy Spirit to help you to successfully complete that particular point according to His Spirit.

Make sure your heart is open and honest before Him. After you have finished that specific point, give God a prayer of praise, thanksgiving and worship for hearing you, accepting you, and for totally releasing you from that point, and then proceed to the next step. The following are some guidelines that may help assist you in implementing each of the seven points we have named above.

1. Ask God to Forgive You For Your Sins

Begin by asking God to forgive you for your sins in general. Next, you are to inventory your heart, life and your actions to see if there is anything current in your life that needs to be dealt with. David did this when he asked the Lord, *"Search my heart O God, and see if there is any wickedness in me."* When you search your heart, God is going to show you things—big things and little things. As you find them, repent of them, and ask for God's hand of deliverance and His help to overcome them.

You are then to ask the Holy Spirit to search your heart for the specific sin that may have caused the curse. If you cannot find the specific sin, spend some time crying out to the Lord for repentance. Do not rush this point. Sometimes God wants us to go through a mourning period for our sins. This is something that may take days or even weeks. Once you sense in your spirit that God has released you, you can then go to the next step.

If you need some help with this prayer, we have several prayers in Volume 1 of *"The Weapons of Our Warfare"* that may assist you. The two prayers that may be of assistance to you are the prayer of the 51st Psalm and the prayer asking for forgiveness for sin. These prayers were not specifically written for the repentance of sins regarding generational curses, but they deal with repenting and asking for God's forgiveness.

2. Repent For the Sins of Your Ancestors

This section was also covered in chapter ten, but I want to also reemphasize this area. Because you are repenting for the sins of your ancestors, you may not know what the specific sin was that caused the curse. In this area, God is not requiring that you know the specific sin, but that you cry out and repent to Him for your ancestors' sins.

In chapter ten we talked about how we must repent for the sins of our nation. Even though we may not have personally committed the types of sins and abominations that have spiritually and morally corroded our nation, we are to still cry out to God for His mercy and forgiveness on behalf of our nation as a whole.

In the same manner, you may not have committed the sins for which your ancestors are guilty, but you are still to cry out to God on behalf of the sins of your ancestors. As we said in chapter ten, and again in the above topic, this is something that you cannot rush. If God is judging you for something your ancestors did, it is either a sin in which they did not repent, or it was a sin in which they did not repent of adequately. As we said in the previous topic, sometimes God wants us to spend some time mourning and crying out to Him for our sins. You must continue to do this until you get a release in your spirit that God has accepted your repentance.

3. Forgive Others
4. Release Others

I placed these two points together because of their similarity. In chapter ten we detailed how they are different. But the way you overcome them is the same. You do it through prayer. Until you are able to totally forgive and release them, add them to your prayer list and begin praying for them. The more you pray for them, the more the walls of unforgiveness and offense will become broken down in your heart—allowing the spirit of forgiveness and release to take place.

Even though you may be tempted to rush through this point, be careful to not rush it. As we discovered, releasing a person from an offense is a matter of the heart. It is not determined by any specific time, but rather, a release of the heart that comes through prayer, and the spirit of God's mercy and grace.

5. Apologize to Others that You Have Offended

It is extremely vital for you to commit this point to prayer. It is always essential to pray and ask for God's presence and grace to be upon you whenever you must confront someone about a matter that may be difficult or unpleasant. After you commit and consecrate this point to the Lord, ask Him to set the atmosphere for the meeting. Ask for His grace to be upon your words, and that He would lead and guide you in the words you speak. Also ask Him to prepare the heart of the person you are going to speak to so that their heart will be open and receptive to receive what you are about to say.

In Volume 2 of *"The Weapons of Our Warfare,"* there is an excellent prayer that will go with this point. It is entitled, *"When You Need to Confront Someone."* It is just for this type of occasion. If you have this book, pray this prayer before meeting the person.

If they do not receive your apology, give God thanks and praise for giving you the humility, courage and boldness to face the person and confess your fault to them. Even though they did not accept your apology and give you their release, ask God to accept your apology on their behalf and to give you His release from it in spite of their refusal.

Continue to pray for them periodically that the Lord would also bless them to be able to release it. You must pray for them because even though God will release you from the curse even without their release, their refusal to release you will allow the spirit of the Gibeonites to judge them and continue to bring curses and hindrances in their lives.

As we discussed in chapter ten, if they will not release you from the curse, you are then required to give a double atonement offering.

6. Make an Atonement Fast

As with any fast, you must pray and consecrate this fast to the Lord before you begin. In your prayer of consecration, let the Lord know that you are sanctifying this fast unto Him for the atonement of the sin-curse against you or your family. You must also be faithful and diligent in prayer throughout the fast.

Be careful not to over-commit this fast. The reason why I emphasize that you should not over-commit it is because if you break the fast, you must start the fast all over again. Because everyone is at a different level of fasting, I suggest that you carefully pray—asking the Lord what type of fast He would accept. However, do not be so quick to jump to the easier fasts. Remember, no pain, no gain. Also remember, David would not offer God an offering that was not costly to him. Likewise, you should not offer God a fast that does not cost you something.

During this seven day fast you can undergo the entire seven days with the same type of fast, or you can combine several fasts within the seven days. For example, you may begin the first 4 days with the partial fast, which allows you to eat certain foods, and then end the last three days with either the Normal Fast or the Juice Fast. But whichever you (prayerfully) choose, make sure you are faithful and diligent to complete it.

I strongly suggest obtaining our book entitled, *"The Warfare of Fasting"* before undergoing your fast. It will teach you how to fast with the right heart, attitude and spiritual understanding about fasting.

7. Make an Atonement Offering

I would also like to reemphasize the caution we gave in chapter eleven regarding the atonement offering. Make sure you do not merely subtract from your regular tithes and offerings to give the atonement offering. This is to be an additional sacrificial offering. If you simply shuffle money, God will not accept the offering. Once again, it was only after David paid the "full price" that God released Him from the curse. If you do not have the money at this time, wait a while and save it up. If you are truly unable to give this amount without utter destruction to your finances and well-being, then pray and ask the Lord about giving the *"Lesser Way Out"* as we discussed in chapter eleven.

Also as we discussed in chapter eleven, be prayerful as who you are to give this offering. And when you give it, as the scripture tells us, do not give it grudgingly. Give it with a cheerful and thankful heart—knowing that it represents the complete and final payment of the atonement for your sins or your family's sins, and that your deliverance is on the way.

Closing Prayer

After you have totally completed all seven steps, close with the following prayer, receive and declare your victory, liberty and freedom from the curse, and praise Him for your release.

Father, I am thankful to You for Your Son, and our Lord, Jesus Christ, who paid the eternal price and atonement for my sins and the sins of my family. As I have offered up these seven things before You, I pray that you would now accept and receive them as the physical, earthly atonement for my sins and the sins of my ancestors.

Father, when David paid the full price for the sins of Saul and his generation to the Gibeonites (in 2 Samuel chapter 21), you released he and the Israelites from the curse of the famine that was against them. And yet again, when David paid the (full price) atonement for the plague that was against he and his people (in 2 Samuel chapter 24), once again You forgave them and released them from the curse of the plague that was upon them.

Father, Your Word says that You are without respect of persons. I therefore pray that as I have offered these seven things— representing the seven sons of Saul, which also represents the full price as an atonement for my sins and the sins of my ancestors, as you accepted David's atonement and released he and his people from the curses against them, I thank You for also accepting my atonement and releasing my family and me from the curses against us.

And, by my faith in Your Word, and my obedience to Your Word, I decree that I have been set free, and the chains of this generational curse are now broken! I decree this not by my might, nor by my power, but by Your Spirit, the power of Your Word, Your abundant goodness and mercy, and Your ever-loving kindness towards me.

Now Father, I give You, and You alone, all the praise, worship, glory, honor, adoration and thanksgiving for setting me free. And now, in the matchless name of Jesus Christ, I now receive my freedom, liberty and deliverance from this curse. Amen!

Conclusion

> *Thou shalt not bow down thyself to them, nor serve them: for I the LORD thy God am a jealous God, visiting the iniquity of the fathers upon the children unto the third and fourth generation of them that hate me;*
> *Exodus 20:5*

> *And showing mercy unto thousands of them that love me, and keep my commandments.   Exodus 20:6*

The above passage is one of the foundational passages we have used in this book. It clearly shows God's judgment of curses (personal and generational) to those who disobey and rebel against Him. But as we end this book, I want to show you something else in this passage. Although verse 5 shows us the judgment of God that comes from our disobedience, verse 6 contrasts verse 5 by showing us the mercy of God that comes through our obedience.

It says that God shows His mercy to those who love Him and keep His commandments. Even though God sends the curses, He is the same God who actually counteracts the curses He sends against those who disobey Him with a release from the curse that comes through our obedience.

By following the biblical precepts I have outlined through this book (to get released from curses in your life and family), it is demonstrating your act of obedience in keeping the commandments of God, thus opening the door for you to receive God's grace and mercy, and receive your deliverance and release from curses.

After reading this book, you can walk away with one of two concepts: The first is to continue to ignore God's Word, and believe that personal and generational curses do not exist, and continue to suffer famines in your life—wondering when will they ever end. The second is to understand that through the biblical precepts I have shown through this book, that personal and generational curses do exist, and that you may be a victim of one or some of them. Once you come to this understanding, you can then come to the understanding that you do not have to continue to suffer them because God has mercifully given you a way of escape.

If you choose the first (ignore God's Word, and not believe in curses), you are going to continue to experience verse 5—which is to suffer and experience the judgment of God through curses and spiritual famines in your life. If you choose the second, which is to believe that they do exist, and be willing to act upon what you have now come to learn and understand, you will receive verse 6—God's mercy, forgiveness, and a release from the curses of your life.

Once David discovered that he and the Israelites were under a curse, and also understood what he must do in order to get deliverance from the curse, he didn't hesitate to do what he needed to do in order to get deliverance.

Hebrews 13:8 says that *God is the same yesterday, today, and forever*. He is the same God that delivered David from his curses. And, He is the same God that is ready, willing and able to also deliver you from the curses of your life.

If you are willing to do like David and offer the seven sons of Saul (do the seven things required), then you are on your way to getting generational chains broken from your life and experiencing the true liberty, freedom, deliverance and blessings that the Lord intended for you.

Other Books and Materials
By Kenneth Scott

The Weapons Of Our Warfare, Volume 1
This is a handbook of scriptural based prayers for just about every need in your life. There are prayers for your home, marriage, family and many personal issues that we face in our lives each day. If you desire to be developed in prayer, then this is a must book for you.

The Weapons Of Our Warfare, Volume 2
It is a sequel of Volume I, and brings the prayer warrior into the ministry of intercession. It has prayers for your church, pastor, city, our nation, and many other national issues in which we should pray for. If you desire to be developed as an intercessor, then this book is for you.

The Weapons Of Our Warfare, Volume 3
(Confessing God's Word Over Your Life)
There is a difference between prayer and confession. This book gives the believer understanding about confessions and what they do in your life. It also contains daily confessions for major areas of your life. If you have Volumes 1 & 2, then you also need Volume 3.

The Weapons Of Our Warfare, Volume 4
(Prayers for Teens and Young Adults)
Teenagers have different needs than adults. This is a prayer handbook that keeps the same fervency and fire as Volumes 1 & 2, but also addresses the needs of teens. This book is a "must" for your teens.

The Weapons Of Our Warfare Volumes 1 ,2 & 3 on CD
Meditate on the Word of God as it is prayed on audio CDs. These CDs contain prayers from Volumes 1 2, & 3 (sold separately). As you hear these prayers prayed, you can stand in the spirit of agreement and apply them in the spirit to your life, situations and circumstances as you ride in your car, or as you sit in your home. In the Vol 3 Confession series Pastor Scott will lead you in confessions, allowing you to easily follow and quote them afterwards. These CDs are a must for every Christian library.

When All Hell Breaks Loose
Most mature Christians can survive a casual trial here and there, but many of God's people fall during the storms of life. Get this book and learn how to prevail through the storm *"When all Hell Breaks Loose."*

Praying in Your Divine Authority
Many Christians are hindered and defeated by Satan simply because they do not know the dominion and authority they have in Christ. This book teaches the believer how to bind and loose Satan and demon spirits, and how to pray and walk in our divine authority.

The Warfare of Fasting
In Matthew 27:14 Jesus said that some spiritual strongholds, hindrances and bondages will only be broken through prayer and fasting. This book teaches the believer the different types of fasts, the methods of fasting, and the warfare of what happens in the spiritual realm when we fast. If you want to see "total" deliverance in your life, you need to get this book.

Standing In The Gap
In this book Pastor Scott teaches life-changing principles of what it means to make up the hedge, stand in the gap, stand in agreement, and intercede for others. If you are a prayer warrior, an intercessor, or you have a desire to be one, this book is a "must" for you.

Chains That Bind Generations
Do generational curses actually exist? Where do they come from? Does God send generational curses upon my life, or are they from the devil? Could it be that some of my difficulties and struggles in life come from generational curses? If there is a curse on my life or family, can it be broken? Using the life of David, Pastor Scott answers these and other questions about generational curses and teaches you how to get set free and receive your deliverance from generational curses.

The Witchcraft of Profanity
When people use profanity, they think they are simply speaking empty, vain words. These words are not vain at all. They are actually witchcraft spells, evoking demon spirits upon their life and the lives of those they speak over. Get this book for yourself and for others, and learn what's actually going on in the spiritual realm when profanity is used. Once you read this book, you will never use profanity again!

The Basics of Prayer — Understanding The Lord's Prayer
Just about all of us have prayed "The Lord's Prayer," and even know The Lord's Prayer by memory. But very few of us really understand the depths of what Jesus was truly teaching His disciples in this prayer outline. This book gives the believer a scripture by scripture breakdown of this prayer and gives illumination and insight on its understanding.

visit us on the web at www.prayerwarfare.com for inspiring CD messages and other available materials.

Contact Us:

For prayer requests, questions or comments, write to:

Spiritual Warfare Ministries
Attention: Kenneth Scott
P.O. Box 2024
Birmingham, Alabama 35201-2024

(205) 853-9509

Web Site: www.spiritualwarfare.cc
email us at sprwarfare@aol.com

This book is not available in all bookstores. To order additional copies of this book, please send $10.99 plus $2.98 shipping and handling to the above address.

God has anointed Pastor Scott to teach and preach on the power of prayer. If you are interested in him coming to minister at your church or organization, please contact him at the information above.